ARTHURIAN ROMANCE
and
MODERN POETRY AND MUSIC

KING ARTHUR, FRENCH MEDIEVAL TAPESTRY

ARTHURIAN ROMANCE
and
MODERN POETRY AND MUSIC

By

WILLIAM ALBERT NITZE

KENNIKAT PRESS
Port Washington, N. Y./London

ARTHURIAN ROMANCE AND MODERN POETRY AND MUSIC

First published in 1940
Reissued in 1970 by Kennikat Press
Library of Congress Catalog Card No: 72-105816
ISBN 0-8046-1049-5

Manufactured by Taylor Publishing Company   Dallas, Texas

To the Memory of

HARRIET MONROE

FOREWORD

THE chapters of this little book were originally composed as lectures which I gave at the Art Institute in Chicago. They are reprinted here with only such revision as was needed to make them available for the general reader. They make no pretense at treating the stories associated with King Arthur fully or even adequately. My object was to illustrate in a kaleidoscopic fashion the present by means of the past: to suggest how a great poetic tradition has been built up and survives as an essential part of our Western culture. Poetry is here used in its general sense as opposed to historic fact. Several of the works described are in prose. Likewise, by music I refer not to musical scores but to the use by musicians, especially Wagner, of Arthurian imaginative motifs.

The few notes at the end of each chapter express my indebtedness to other scholars. They also offer information of a specific character to those of my readers who may wish to supplement or verify what I have to say.

Harriet Monroe, to whose memory I dedicate this book, used to wonder why our American poet Edwin Arlington Robinson should have succumbed to the spell of Lancelot and Tristan—when the actual American scene appeared so pressing. If my book helps to explain away this difficulty, I shall be satisfied. The core of Harriet Monroe's life was the zest for adventure. She needed no promptings from legends about Arthur, no reminder from Camelot or Tintagel! But she would have been the last to deny the value of a great and beautiful tradition: the *ambages pulcerrimae Arturi regis*, as Dante called the Arthurian legend.

TABLE OF CONTENTS

LIST OF ILLUSTRATIONS

I

AVALON AND THE PASSING OF ARTHUR

WHO in America today remembers the legendary Avalon, or, if he does, cares anything
about it? Who bothers about King Arthur
or in what manner he passed from the scene in which
centuries of Englishmen imagined that he had lived?
Perhaps you will say, "Our children"—some of whom
surely finger and perhaps read Christmas books dealing
with Arthur and the Round Table. As a matter of
fact, they probably read much more exciting things,
the Oz series or Mary Poppins, and as lusty young
Americans they can hardly be blamed. Mark Twain's
A Connecticut Yankee at King Arthur's Court (1889) is still
on the shelves of our public libraries. But does anyone
read it now? And, if so, take seriously the type of
humor it contains? The book is a landmark, but it is
"dated."

Yet in England, or rather Britain, no figure has held
public interest more consistently than Arthur. On
this showing Julius Caesar and even Cromwell sink

1

into the background. Only the Devil—that Puritan
mentor—is more often named in British local tradition
than Arthur. There is Arthur's Castle, Arthur's Oven,
Arthurstone, his Hill, his Quoit, his Fountain, and,
of course, his Tomb—variously located. Surrounded
by his court of gallant knights and fair ladies, King
Arthur has exercised a fascination over writers, and
especially poets, which extends from the period of the
Angevin monarchs in the twelfth century down to the
present age, not to mention the role he plays in the
Welsh *mabinogion* or "literature taught the bard's ap-
prentice," according to Welsh custom. Even John
Milton once planned to write an Arthurian epic, in
which he would tell "of those great-hearted champions
bound in the invisible society of the Round Table." A
legend that is so persistent has in it elements which
are of transcendent value; that is to say, elements
rooted in the genius or the ethos of the nation itself.
As long as there is a British nation, compounded of
Norman, Saxon, and Celtic strains, so long will there
be an Arthurian legend!

In order to realize this we need go back no further
than 1869. In that year Alfred Tennyson published the
first nearly complete edition of the *Idylls of the King*.
Here, in exquisite blank verse, is told for the Victorian
reader the entire Arthurian story as it had come down

to the English from Geoffrey of Monmouth in the twelfth century and Thomas Malory in the fifteenth, embellished by Tennyson's readings in Welsh literature—proceeding from Arthur's miraculous birth, through his coronation, his festive gathering of knights (Sir Bedivere, Sir Kay, Sir Gawain, and others), his battles with foreign foes, his betrayal by Modred and Guenevere, down to his last battle and defeat, and finally his 'passing' to Avalon. We should look in vain in Tennyson for that "sort of cloudy Stonehenge grandeur" which Edward Fitzgerald had expected to find. But there were compensations. The Victorian age was rapidly approaching its zenith. The abortive February revolutions, so disquieting for Germany and France, had left scarce a ripple in English political life. The dedication of the *Idylls* to the memory of the Prince Consort (he died in 1861) looks forward to a sturdy race of Hanoverian kings. So that the atmosphere of the *Idylls* is one of smugness and calm, of confidence in England's dynastic stability, in the face of the unsettled world without.

And yet, beneath this peaceful surface runs a note of concern and anxiety as to England's future. Not even in the *Ode to Virgil*, with its magnificent foreboding:

> Thou majestic in thy sadness at the doubtful
> doom of humankind,

is this feeling more acute, or more Virgilian. Listen to
the second-to-last of the poems, *Pelleas and Ettare*
(Lancelot and Guenevere are conversing):

> And each foresaw the dolorous day to be:
> And all talk died, as in a grove all song
> Beneath the shadow of some bird of prey,
> Then a long silence came upon the hall,
> And Modred thought, "The time is hard at hand."

Certainly Tennyson could not have foreseen the cata-
clysm of 1914. He did not know, for all his contact
with statesmen, that England's hour was "hard at
hand." But he had his misgivings, and with subtle
epic power this time he voices his fears in the con-
cluding poem, *The Passing of Arthur* (it is the moment
before the Battle of Camlan):

> Then spake King Arthur to Sir Bedivere,
> "Far other is this battle in the West
> Whereto we move, than when we strove in youth
> And thrust the heathen from the Roman wall,
> And shook them thro' the north. Ill doom is mine
> To war against my people and my knights,
> The king who fights his people fights himself.
> . . . .
> The sequel of today unsolders all
> The goodliest fellowship of famous knights
> Whereof the world holds record. Such a sleep
> They sleep—the men I loved. I think that we
> Shall never more, at any future time,
> Delight our souls with talk of knightly deeds,

Walking about the gardens and the halls
Of Camelot, as in the days that were.
I perish by this people which I made—
Tho' Merlin swore that I should come again
To rule once more—."

In the operatic scene that follows the battle—when
Arthur is carried away to Avalon—he utters a fare-
well, not as heartbreaking as that of Wotan in Wagner's *Walküre*, but just as majestic and no less beautiful:

"I am going a long way
With these thou seëst—if indeed I go
(For all my mind is clouded with a doubt)
To the island-valley of Avilion,
Where falls not hail, or rain, or any snow,
Nor ever wind blows loudly, but it lies
Deep-meadow'd, happy, fair with orchard-lawns
And bowery hollows crown'd with summer sea;
Where I will heal me of my grievous wound."

The passages quoted represent England, the home of
Arthurian story, as Tennyson thought of her in his
prophetic foreshadowings about the middle of the
nineteenth century. Arthur and Avalon—out of the
tradition of the past he had seized the two motifs that
gave life to the myth. Before tracing these to their
lair in early British and Roman sources, let us—as a
contrast—glance for a moment across the Channel to
Germany.

There, in 1860, another poet—a more dynamic one—was struggling with his own *Götterdämmerung*. Richard Wagner also had his Arthurian background: Tannhäuser, Tristan, Lohengrin, and Parsifal. Only in Germany the subject was not native. It was borrowed from France in medieval times, and in Wagner's teeming imagination it had become fused with earth-born Teutonic tradition, the Nibelungen and the Eddas. In Wagner's half-forgotten "Wibelungen Essay" of 1848 this fusion is already made in the most astonishing way: the Nibelungen Hoard is also the Grail, Frederick Barbarossa is Arthur and also Siegfried, and Siegfried is Baldur, later Parsifal, and Baldur is Christ.

Says Wagner's recent biographer, Ernest Newman:

> It is almost impossible to condense the nebulous haze of Wagner's argument . . . . into lucid statement in any other language [than German]. His interpretation of history is often fantastic. . . . . One asks oneself in wonder what all his reasoning has to do with the serious business of writing operas. . . . . The answer is that Wagner had in 1848 arrived at a stage when he could take up no subject without bringing to bear upon it the whole might of his extraordinarily active brain, of his wide reading, and of his troubled spiritual experience.

The truth is that, unlike Tennyson, Wagner was the immediate product of the generation of 1848; Wagner was a born revolutionist, in everything else as well as in music. His romantic soul was compounded of all the strains, emotional and intellectual, that go with the word 'freedom'—freedom from the Babbitts who through their *Kleingeisterei* had divided Germany against herself; freedom from property, the curse of the Nibelungen and of capitalism; freedom in love from the shackles of bourgeois morality; and lastly, in *Parsifal*, freedom from self. That is why, over and over again in his work—beginning with *The Flying Dutchman*—he stresses the motif that death alone can set the human being free. In short, while the aristocratic Tennyson, ensconced in his ivory tower, pensively questions the passage of a great age, the revolutionist Wagner tears his troubled, romantic soul into resounding threads—until, at the age of seventy, it floats over into the serene and majestic music of his last opera, *Parsifal*.

Now, such a comparison has its uses. It differentiates not only individuals, but civilizations, and the respective media, poetry and music, in which they express themselves. But it does something more: it reveals the extraordinary vitality and pliability of the Matter of Britain—as the Middle Ages called the Arthurian legend itself. Finally, it makes clear that in its national significance as epic the Matter of Britain, as its name implies, remains British from the earliest times down to the present. This in spite of the fact that other nationals have exploited it—Wolfram von Eschenbach and Wagner in Germany, Chrétien de Troyes and an unknown Cistercian in France, and recently Edwin Arlington Robinson in America; and these are only the really great names.

This brings us back to Britain. Who was King Arthur? And where is, or rather was, the "island-valley of Avilion" or Avalon, whence Merlin expected the British king to return?

We begin with a second-century Latin inscription from far-off Dalmatia. It was found on an ornate *arca* or 'coffin' near Split, the former Spalato, on the Adriatic. It records the career, in biographical form, of a famous Roman soldier, Artorius Castus, whose main exploit took place in Britain. Rendered into current English, this is what it says:

> Lucius Artorius the Incorruptible offers prayers to the Gods of the Lower World (his household deities), and while still living dedicates this tablet to himself and his family. He was centurion or captain in four Roman legions; to wit, the Third Gallica, the Sixth Ferrata, the Second Adjutrix, and the Fifth Macedonica. Likewise he was ranking centurion of the last-mentioned legion and became commander of the fleet lying off Misenum (Naples). Then he was colonel of the Sixth Victrix Legion (stationed at York in Britain) and as *dux* or 'leader' headed an expedition of British infantry and cavalry auxiliaries against the Armoricans (in Gaul). Finally, he became imperial collector of the province of Liburnia (Northern Dalmatia) with power of life and death.

This page from a Roman *Who's Who* is tantalizingly succinct. The more so since ancient writers on Britain, including Suetonius, never breathe Artorius' name. And yet the family name *Artorius* is our later common name Arthur, and therefore that of King Arthur. Why did historians ignore him? Perhaps for the reason that, although a successful soldier under the emperor Hadrian, he abstained from politics; the epithet 'incorruptible' (*castus*) may be significant. But the mention of the British campaign and specifically the reference to the very important Sixth Legion provide us with a valuable clue.

The Sixth Legion was renowned in Roman military history as *victrix* ('victorious'), *pia* ('patriotic'), and *fidelis* ('loyal'). During the reigns of Hadrian and Antoninus Pius it was stationed in Britain. That was in the second century of the Christian Era—the period when the Roman sway was carried farthest north in the British Isles, and Hadrian built the Roman Wall (*murum*), which ran from Carlisle to Newcastle-upon-Tyne, to be followed after A.D. 138 by the construction of the Antonine Wall (*vallum*), extending from the mouth of the Clyde to the Firth of Forth. As we know from numerous inscriptions recently discovered, the Sixth Legion took an active and notable part in both of these undertakings. We also know that the main body of the Sixth Legion occupied a strategic position at York on the military road leading to the north. But—once more—no Latin inscription found in Britain mentions Artorius or the expedition against the Armoricans, although, as the historian Mommsen has observed, this is no reason for doubting the veracity of the events recorded on the Dalmatian *arca*.

Such, in barest outline, are the facts. What inferences can we draw from them? First, that there existed a Roman *dux* or 'leader' by the name of Arthur; second, that he commanded in Britain one of the most important legions of the Empire; and, third, that during his sojourn in Britain the Romans drove back the native tribes of the north and strongly fortified themselves against them, though the exploit of which he himself was proudest was the Armorican war.

The passing of Roman Britain is still one of the great historical mysteries. In the words of a recent historian: "There is an almost complete absence of written records for the British Isles between A.D. 400 and 550. Darkness hangs over them, and the mists of Arthurian legend." We must skip to the eighth century to get another significant mention of Arthur. Referring to the Saxon invaders, the Harleian manuscript (containing Nennius' "History of the Britons" of that

date) reports in what may possibly be the remnant of
a Latin poem:

> Tunc Arthur pugnabat contra illos in illis diebus
> Cum regibus Brittonum, sed ipse dux erat bellorum.
>
> Then Arthur fought against the Saxons in those days
> Together with the British kings, but he himself was a
> leader in battles.

These lines clearly mean that Arthur was not himself
regarded as a king but as a *dux* or 'commander in battle.' Apparently he was still known by the old, Roman title. Of the battles then enumerated by the
manuscript up to the traditional number of twelve, it
has been possible to identify only some five or six, but
all these except one can be located within striking dis-
tance of the walls built by Hadrian and Antoninus
Pius. It should be noted also that two hundred years
later the "Annals of Wales" mention an additional
battle—that of Camlan—which they assign to the
year 537. "In this battle," say the Annals, "both
Arthur and Modred fell (*in qua Arthur et Medraut cor-
ruerunt*)."

Thus, after the lapse of centuries, the person of
Arthur reappears—in written documents, still as a
'leader' in battles on the borderland between England
and Scotland, but now represented as the champion of
the British against the conquering Saxon horde. But

if this Arthur be identical with the hero of the Dalmatian inscription, how was his fame handed down to later ages? We do not know. What we do know, however, is that across the Channel in France the Roland (*Hruodlandus*) mentioned by Einhard in his "Life of Charlemagne" is the same person as the epic hero of the *Chanson de Roland*, some three centuries later. The parallel is interesting because it shows how the shift from history to epic legend or saga must have occurred. Historically Roland was a 'count' of the March of Brittany; he fell in an engagement with the Basques in 778. In the epic he reappears as the count of Brittany, but the battle in which he died is now waged against the Saracens, the national foes of the French, and the period (1086) is that preceding the First Crusade. So it is with Arthur: the historical fact is that the troops under his leadership fought against the northern British around A.D. 150; some time after the sixth century epic legend transformed Arthur into a British leader engaged in the defense of England against the Saxons.

In both cases the epic conception is a national one: Roland, a Frankish hero, becomes a Frenchman; and Arthur, a Roman, is henceforth claimed by the British imagination as its own.

But the most important change, to complete the epic

fiction, was to follow. It came when, after the Norman Conquest of England (1066), the Norman-Angevin dynasty, under the first two Henrys, needed support. The reign of King Stephen was a tragic interlude. Stephen himself, from the dynastic point of view, was a weak interloper, and his reign was marred by disastrous civil war. But early in his reign Geoffrey of Monmouth published (1136–38) his *Historia regum Britanniae*, in which Arthur appears as 'King' Arthur, a world-conqueror similar to Alexander and Charlemagne, and the Arthurian story assumes dynamic form. "No work of the imagination," says Sir Edmund Chambers, "save the *Aeneid*, has done more to shape the legend of a people than the *Historia*." Certainly no Englishman, aware of Britain's destiny, can question that remark. In surveying the British scene from the Roman occupation to the triumph of the Saxons, including the exile of the last British or Celtic ruler, Cadwallader, Geoffrey had one end in view. It was to exalt Arthur—now King Arthur—as the founder of English monarchy and the exemplar of Roman-British culture, as Geoffrey beheld it through the lens of twelfth-century chivalry. Thus, Geoffrey gave body to the Arthurian epic, and on the fictional side he created the Arthurian *romance*, which was to sweep Europe.

What Geoffrey wished to suggest was that the ruling Norman house—descending in the person of Henry I—is the future dynasty which Merlin had in mind when, in the *Historia*, he is made to prophesy the return of Arthur from Avalon (whither he had gone "to be healed of his wounds," *ad sananda vulnera sua*). Geoffrey had two strings to his bow: with the one he gave the Norman usurpers an ancestry in Roman-British tradition; with the other he flattered the Celts by assuring them that the Saxon domination was ended (as under the Conqueror it actually was) and that England was once more to return to legitimate British rule. The potency of this suggestion did not fail to strike home. Later English monarchs, among them Elizabeth, were alive to its appeal.

But if it was Geoffrey's kudos to further the dynastic and national cause, it was the pageantry of chivalric life and custom as reflected in the court at Caerleon (later Camelot) that gave the *Historia* its romantic appeal. Into it, as a framework, later writers on the Continent and in England introduced other poetic themes dealing with Lancelot, Perceval, Galahad, and the Holy Grail. Notable, in this regard, is the addition of the Round Table—as a knightly institution or order—by Geoffrey's French translator, the Norman poet Wace. Yet Geoffrey himself was responsible for the two important motifs on which later ages were to build. One of these was Guenevere's faithlessness to Arthur. Guenevere (Welsh *Gwenhwyfar*, Irish *Finnabair*) means 'faireyebrow'; she appears to be of mythical origin and she is irresistible to mortals. Geoffrey made Modred her paramour, thus the betrayer of Arthur, slain by the King in his last great battle at Camlan. How later medieval taste replaced him by Lancelot will be treated in another chapter. Suffice it here to add that in stressing this motif Geoffrey set the stage for all subsequent Lancelot and Tristan romances.

More significant, however, is the value Geoffrey attached to the Avalon or return motif. Again, *Avalon* is of Celtic derivation; the word means 'apple orchard,' the equivalent of the classical 'garden of Hesperides.' And the theme itself was dear to the Celts, who believed—as they still do today—that the *sid*-folk entice heroes to the Happy Otherworld "beyond the waves," whence at a destined moment they return to earth to fight. The Irish Book of Leinster (1150) preserves this idea in an earlier Gaelic form. There the hero is Fraech, not Arthur. Nevertheless, the theme must have been familiar to Geoffrey, although the details of the Irish story do not recur until Layamon, Geoffrey's imitator, reproduced them. Here is the version as the Irishman tells it—after Fraech has been grievously wounded:

> Then they [Fraech's attendants] heard something—a wailing upon Cruachan. There were seen thrice fifty women with purple tunics, with green headdresses, with pins of silver on their wrists. A messenger is sent . . . . to learn what they lamented.
>
> "Fraech, son of Idath," says the woman, "the darling of the king of the fairy-hills of Ireland." At this, Fraech hears the wailing. "Lift me out," says he to his retinue; "this is the weeping . . . . of the women of Boand." Upon that he is lifted out and carried to them . . . . and they carry him away into the fairy-hill of Cruachan.
>
> At the time of nones on the morrow this is what they saw: he comes and he is quite whole, without stain and without blemish, and fifty women around him, equal in age, in figure, in beauty, in fairness, in symmetry, in form. . . . .
>
> Thereupon Fraech goes into the dun. All the folk rise to meet him and welcome him as if it were from another world he came.

The similarity of this tale to the description of Arthur in Avalon, as retold by Layamon and Malory (whom Tennyson follows), needs little demonstration. As Malory describes the scene:

> Sir Bedivere took the king upon his back, and so went with him to the water side. And when they were at the water side, even by the bank hovered a little barge with many fair ladies in it, and among them all was the queen, and all they had black hoods, and all they wept and shrieked when they saw King Arthur. Now put me into the barge, said the king. And so he did softly; and there received him three queens with great mourning;

and so they set them down, and in one of their laps King Arthur laid his head. And then that queen said: Ah, dear brother, why have ye tarried so long from me? alas, this wound on your head hath caught over-much cold. And so then they rowed from the land, and Sir Bedivere beheld all those ladies go from him.

Like Fraech, the British king is borne to a fairy abode to be healed of his wounds; like Fraech, hooded women bemoan his departure; like Fraech, he will return some day to rule again. In capitalizing this idea of the return, Geoffrey of Monmouth gave to the 'passing' of Arthur its imperishable note, and to the British nation a symbol of their faith in kingship.

It is always difficult in literature to make goodness credible. The figure of the British king must have no blemish. As Tennyson saw, in the fierce light that beats upon a throne Arthur (or Albert, Victoria's consort) had to be impeccable,

> Wearing the white flower of a blameless life.

Tennyson, the poet, has many shortcomings. But his treatment of Arthur is not one of them. Doing no evil nor thinking it, exemplary in manners, anxious to help his people but holding aloof from them; blameless, guileless, irreproachable; sprung from the loins of a dim, shadowy Artorius Castus—his Arthur remains true to the Galfridian tradition, perhaps "clouded with a doubt," but destined all the same to be the rallying ground of the British race: Celt, Norman, Saxon. That is why poetry may be truer to life than history. That is why so many generations of Englishmen have loved and cherished the legendary figure of King Arthur.

On Arthur in general see E. K. Chambers, *Arthur of Britain* (London: Sidgewick & Jackson, 1927).

On Tennyson see *Life and Works* (10 vols.; New York: Macmillan, 1889), including the *Memoir by His Son.*

On Wagner see Ernest Newman, *The Life of Richard Wagner* (New York: Knopf, 1937), especially Vol. II—a monumental contribution.

On Artorius see Kemp Malone, *Modern Philology*, XXII (1924–25), 367–74, and the confirmation by Thurneysen, *Zeitschrift für celtische Philologie*, XX (1933), 136.

On Nennius see Arthur G. Brodeur, "Arthur, *Dux Bellorum*," *University of California Publications in English*, III (1939), 237–84.

The inscription given on p. 8 follows Malone's interpretation of the *Corpus inscriptionum Latinarum*, III, 303, No. 1919. If the reader is interested in delving further into the history of the Sixth Legion, he should consult Sir George MacDonald, *The Roman Wall in Scotland* (2d ed.; Oxford: Clarendon Press, 1934).

On the 'passing' of Arthur and the Fraech story see Tom Peete Cross in *The Manly Anniversary Studies* (Chicago: University of Chicago Press, 1923), pp. 284–94.

SITE OF MARK'S CASTLE, TINTAGEL BY THE SEA

II

TRISTAN AND THE LOVE-DEATH MOTIF

IT IS usual nowadays to decry the heroic. In place
of the omniscience of the gods—what the Greeks
called Fate, and the Christians Providence—we
moderns pin our faith to Science. We have become
'realistic' (as we proudly say), and, having stripped
off one illusion after another, we face the economic
illusion that man lives by bread alone. Nevertheless,
the mystery of life still haunts us with terror and wonder. Innumerable things have been said of Tristan
and Isolt by competent and gifted authors: Thomas of
England, Gottfried von Strassburg, Hans Sachs, Malory
—of course, Wagner, Swinburne, Morris, Robinson,
and Erskine. But the essential thing about their
story will always be the helplessness of the three main
characters in it (Tristan, Isolt, and Mark) in the face
of a power that none of them can master and that
sweeps them headlong to their doom.

The outlines of the story are familiar enough: How
Tristan came to Ireland to fetch a wife for his uncle,

King Mark of Cornwall; how she turned out to be Isolt, who had healed him of a wound; how through an error they drink the love potion intended for Mark on his wedding night and thus unwillingly are faithless to Mark; how Tristan, torn by remorse, flees to Brittany; and finally how, again wounded in battle, Tristan sends for Isolt but dies before her arrival, whereupon she lies down and dies beside him.

These are the bare facts, but the passion infusing them has made the *Tristan* the greatest love tragedy in literature. It has no parallel in Greek, though it is Greek in its attachment to the sea and in its stark expression of emotion. Here the "Celtic magic"—to borrow Matthew Arnold's term—has wrought a combination of human feeling, of primitive custom and taboo, and of high moral suffering, which, while typical of the early Irish, is unique on the continent of Europe.

These qualities must have been in Wagner's mind when he wrote to Liszt in 1854 about a great change in his artistic point of view. He says he hopes to complete the *Ring* and produce it by 1858. But, he continues, he now has in mind a *Tristan und Isolde*. "Since I have never enjoyed in life the real happiness of love, I will erect to this most beautiful of all dreams a memorial in which, from beginning to end, this love shall for once drink its fill." Eleven years later the *Tristan* was performed under the direction of Hans von Bülow in Munich, where, at the rehearsal, "if a difficult passage went particularly well, Wagner would spring up, embrace or kiss the singer warmly, or out of pure joy stand on his head on the sofa." But Wagner's love was no abstract fiction, no Lady of Shalott who saw life in a mirror. She was, during the whole *Tristan* period, a very real person, Mathilde Wesendonk. He had met the Wesendonks, husband and wife, at Zürich in 1852. His contacts with them at the "Asyll," adjoining the Wesendonk's villa, are well known. Suffice it to repeat that "happy in Mathilde's proximity, and with the *Tristan* rapidly taking shape in him, Wagner felt for a while a new interest and, he assures us, a new courage." An interest, however, that was to be thwarted, as happened to him time and again, by the realization that for him at least real love could never be gratified. Only death could set such love, as he felt and imagined it, free!

The fact is, as so often happens with artists, that Frau Wesendonk was mainly the occasion for his composition of the *Tristan*. That she herself was capable of sharing Wagner's consuming passion in kind seems doubtful. "All that we can be sure of," says Newman, "is that at an early stage of their acquaintance Wagner was greatly attracted by Mathilde, in whom he found a ready listener to his tales of woe." As Frau Wesendonk remarked wistfully in after-years: "I was a blank page for Wagner to write on." Swept off her feet by the great artist's attentions, she suffered the obloquy that her (and her husband's) bourgeois respectability brought with it.

But what was it Wagner wrote upon that "blank page"? What form or forms had the legend of Tristan taken before Wagner became interested in it? The Middle High German version of the *Tristan* by Gottfried von Strassburg was known to the German Romantic school as early as 1785. It had been variously re-edited from medieval manuscripts when in 1844 Hermann Kurz published the first modern German rendition, to be followed in 1855 by Simrock's less successful poetic rendering. Roughly speaking, this was the material from which Wagner's imagination caught fire. But Gottfried's text, while written in the thirteenth century, was itself only a translation or paraphrase of an earlier French version by Thomas of England (about 1170), and this in turn—together with other French, Norse, Czech, and German versions—goes back to a lost original, which medieval poets called the *Estoire de Tristan*. From this corpus of romance, the late

Joseph Bédier reconstructed what he thought was the plot of the original in his delightful *Roman de Tristan et Iseut* in 1900. I shall refer presently to this reconstruction of the story. But before doing so, I wish to say a word about the background, historical and legendary, on which the lost French *Estoire* rests.

The earliest mention historically of the name Tristan (Gaelic *Drostan*) occurs in documents of Scotch or Pictish origin of the eighth century. But history tells us nothing of this hero's passion for the blond-haired Isolt, and it is equally silent about Mark and his Cornish stronghold on the sea at Tintagel. The only historical reference that we have to Mark is a vague tradition of a Cornish king by that name in a saint's life of 884. Nevertheless, the Tristan theme is of Celtic origin. For Irish saga alone, among early literatures, abounds in the type of tragic 'elopements' or *aitheda* (as they were called) in which the Tristan story is unique in England and on the Continent: a situation in which a sister's son, bound to an uncle by every tie of gratitude, against his own will runs off with his benefactor's wife, against her will also; and thus brings about the destruction of all concerned.

Twelve such *aitheda* are still extant in Old Irish manuscripts. Let us examine one of them, the "Elope-

ment of Diarmuid and Grainne,'' preserved in tradi-
tions going back to the tenth century.

The story is that of Diarmuid, nephew of Finn mac Cumhail,
who is one of his uncle's closest friends and most trusted warriors.
Grainne, daughter of Cormac, high king of Ireland, is Finn's af-
fianced wife. But Grainne was given to him in an unlucky hour,
for ''Finn was hateful to the maiden and such was her hatred that
she sickened of it.''

There is in another Irish manuscript a ninth-century
gloss to her love for another, and it runs as follows:

And Grainne sang: ''There is one for a long look from whom I
should be thankful: for whom I would give the whole world, O
Son of Mary, though it be a privation.''

This person is Diarmuid, of whom there was a tradition in Scotland and Ireland that he had a mark on his
cheek, called a 'love spot,' which made him irresistible to any woman who saw it, and of which Grainne
again sang:

> Master and charmer of women,
> Son of O'Duibhne of swift victories,
> Wooing has not lifted her eyes
> Since the clay was placed on his cheek.

But Diarmuid repulsed the woman, saying:

I will not go with thee; I will not take thee in softness, and I
will not take thee in hardness; I will not take thee without, and
I will not take thee within; I will not take thee on horseback, and
I will not take thee on foot.

As in the *Tristan*, Grainne might have had recourse to a love drink, but Irish as she is she puts a 'spell' or *geis* upon the hero to go with her, and a *geis* in Irish is a taboo which, if disregarded, always "entails moral degradation and swift retribution." Thus the twain, Diarmuid and Grainne, are marked by fate for the tragic end. "She is under the spell of the 'love-spot,' and he under the *geis*. They cannot escape. . . . . They cannot defy fate, and subject to it, they must' defy every human tie."

Or, if he prefer, the reader can consult in the modern English rendering by Lady Gregory, the "Fate of the Sons of Usnach," the kernel of which is the "Elopement of Deirdre with Naisi." Here the principals are Conor the king, Deirdre his wife, and Naisi the son of Usnach. The main difference between this tale and that of Grainne is that the retribution falling upon the lovers involves the entire clan of the Usnachs: "Three thousand stout men went with them, and for sixteen years never did they allow cries of lamentation and of fear among the Ulstermen to cease: each night their vengeful forays caused men to quake." But Deirdre lived on for a year with Conor:

During all that time she smiled no smile of laughter, she satisfied not herself with food or with sleep, and she raised not her head from her knee. . . . . One day Conor said to her:

"Whom dost thou hate most of those whom thou seest?" She answered:

"Thee thyself, and with thee Eogan the son of Dubthacht" (who helped Conor to kill Naisi).

"Then," said Conor, "thou shalt dwell with Eogan for a year." And he gave Deidre over into Eogan's hand.

And upon the morrow they went over the festal plain of Mackay, and Deidre sat behind Eogan in the chariot. . . . .Now, there was a great rock of stone in front of them, and Deidre struck her head upon that stone, and she shattered her head, and so she died.

Shadowy as these tales are, and they are made more so by the fragmentary condition in which they have been transmitted—they already embody, three centuries earlier than the *Tristan*, the situation that makes the love story of Tristan and Isolt so overpowering. Even the external symbol of that love, the 'love drink' or philter, is foreshadowed in the 'love spot' and the *geis* of the Irish saga.

When the *Estoire de Tristan* finally emerged, in its Norman-French form (about 1150), it must have had the following fixed traits:

Tristan is now son of the king of Leonois in Brittany (hence his later appellation "Tristan of Lyonesse") and of Blanchefleur, sister of Mark, king of Cornwall. His mother dies in giving him birth, an incident playing upon the word *triste*, *tristan*, and later developed in Malory's *Morte Darthur*. Instructed in knighthood by Gorvenal, a follower of his father, Tristan then goes to Cornwall, where he takes service with his maternal uncle, King Mark.

Now follows the conventional deed of valor which gives the hero his renown. Mark pays an annual tribute to Ireland of every third Cornish child that has reached the age of fifteen, and the Morholt—a monster like Grendel in *Beowulf*—comes yearly to Tintagel to enforce the Irish claim. Tristan wounds him mortally in single combat, but during the exploit he leaves a fragment of his own sword in the Morholt's head and is himself wounded. Having freed his uncle's realm from the Irish tribute, Tristan languishes in illness due to his wound.

Despairing of a cure, he has himself placed in a boat and pushes out to sea—taking his harp along. The boat drifts to Ireland. The Irish king, hearing Tristan play on the harp, pulls him ashore, and the king's daughter, skilled in the art of medicine, heals him. He calls himself "Tantris" and so eludes recognition. He then returns to Cornwall.

Meantime, Mark is importuned by his followers to marry in order to beget an heir. He refuses on the ground that he wishes Tristan to succeed him. One day, when he is hard pressed by his courtiers, a swallow flies into the hall and lets fall some strands of a

woman's hair. Thoughtlessly, Mark proclaims that he
will marry only the woman to whom the hair belongs.
The quest is again intrusted to Tristan, who discovers
—so inexorable is life—that the woman he seeks is
Isolt. How he overcomes a dragon in order to win her
for Mark is purely incidental. More important is the
fact that, before they sail from Ireland, Isolt has
learned through the nick in Tristan's sword and the
fragment in the monster's head that it was Tristan
who had killed her uncle, the Morholt. Thus fate
balks the lovers!

The return of the pair on the ship to Cornwall and
the episode of the love potion have been made memor-
able through Wagner's opera. But let us remember
that Isolt's mother had prepared the 'love drink'
against the chance that King Mark might not approve
her daughter. The paradox in the story is that through
Brangien's mistake the potion is given to Tristan and
Isolt and not to Mark and his bride. And here the Old
French story-teller crystallizes the theme in an epic
formula: When Brangien, realizing her error, cries
out: "Cursed is the day when I was born, for it is death
that you have drunk!"—Tristan, in his heart, knows
that it is not death but freedom, and he utters the triumphant words:

Isolt ma drue, Isolt m'amie!
En vus ma mort, en vus ma vie.

Isolt my troth, Isolt my love!
In you my death, in you my life.

It matters little to us today that the verbal expression employed was borrowed from the *Disciplina clericalis*, a medieval collection of *exempla*. What is significant is that the poet, with that mastery of concentration characteristic of him, grasped the theme in a flash of the imagination and encased it in permanent form. Wagner found these lines in Gottfried and drew from them his inspiration; the entire idea of his *Tristan*—of the entire Tristan story indeed—is in them: the freedom of love in death; in a word, the *Liebestod*.

The other episodes of the *Estoire* can be summarized briefly. They cluster mainly about two points: (*a*) the ruses to which the lovers resort to escape the vigilance of Mark and (*b*) the theme of the second Isolt, she of the White Hands (as the first was Isolt of the Golden Hair), to whom Tristan finally flees in Brittany.

As to the first of these themes, it all depends on how many devices any specific story-teller wishes to employ in order to play off King Mark against Tristan in their respective claims upon Isolt. The various deceits practiced on Mark can be multiplied indefinitely. Again and again Tristan is torn from Isolt, only to be united to her once more in one of those all-too-brief incidents snatched from the watchful spying of their enemies. Besides, Tristan—later termed Sir Tristram—was too popular a personage not to be assimilated to the main corpus of Arthurian story, built upon the framework of Geoffrey of Monmouth, and incorporated in the *Morte Darthur* of Malory. Rising above all these details, however, is the original story-teller's attitude toward King Mark. Obviously the injured party, Mark's dignity and one's sympathy with him were essential features in the epic plot. The author of the *Estoire*—the feature survives in Wagner—grasped the full tragedy of Mark. When at the Metropolitan in New York Melchior sings the part of Tristan (in the scene where Mark, led by Melot, surprises the lovers in the forest), he suddenly lets his voice drop to a speaking tone and tells Mark:

> Und was Du frägst,
> Das kannst Du nie erfahren.

> And what you ask,
> That you can never learn.

The older narrative misses the poignancy that Wagner gave the scene; but it does not fail to suggest its cruelty. Hence, we may assume, the Tristan story—similar in this to its Irish model—once ended with the flight of the lovers into the forest, where Mark killed them.

For better or worse, however, the author of the *Estoire* added two further episodes: Tristan's escape to Brittany, whither Isolt finally follows him, and the meeting of Tristan with the second Isolt—the Isolt of the White Hands. It conformed to Wagner's design to retain the first incident; the second he wisely eliminated though it occurred in his source. Only recently the late Edwin Arlington Robinson has made the second Isolt the main subject of his poem *Tristram* (1927). A word or two about her is thus in place.

The author of the *Estoire* regarded Isolt of the White Hands as a foil to the first Isolt. She becomes a medieval stylistic device: to show that Tristan cannot forget, despite Nature's mirage to deceive him, his one and only attachment. He respects the second Isolt, but he cannot love her—quite aside from the fact that her jealousy has a part in the events leading to his death. To the American poet Robinson, however, she is the really tragic figure in the story. She is the modern frustrated woman. Her drama is that Tristan died for the experience denied herself:

> It was like that
> For women, sometimes, and might be so too often
> For women like her. She hoped there were not many

Of them, or many of them to be, not knowing
More about that than about waves and foam,
And white birds everywhere, flying, and flying;
Alone, with her white face and her gray eyes,
She watched them there till even her thoughts were white,
And there was nothing alive but white birds flying,
Flying, and always flying, and still flying,
And the white sunlight flashing on the sea.

Clearly, Robinson has pathos, and his lyric gift is unmistakable. But Robinson was thinking of himself; his own life was a tangle of frustrations, like the New England from which he came. The result is that his heroine is a hapless, sickly creature, an anticlimax to the fiery Irish queen of the medieval poet and of Wagner. Wagner's instinct was right: the *Tristan* had no room for shadows or defeatists. And, if love meant surrender and death, it also meant liberation for those to whom life—in the material sense—is merely a physical and social encumbrance. I stress the idea again because nowadays it is often misunderstood. The *Liebestod* is not annihilation; it is joy and freedom. It is the paean of all who have really felt.

Never did Wagner's intellectual power appear to greater advantage than in shaping the scenario of this opera. In a burst of certainty he cut through the intricacies of the Tristan saga and selected its great dramatic moments:

1. The family feud of the lovers, due to the social barriers that separate them. Hence, early in the plot, he lets Isolde chant the threnody:

> Mir erkoren, mir verloren,
> Hehr und heil, kühn und feig,
> Todgeweihtes Haupt.

> Won for me, lost to me,
> Hale and sound, brave and cowardly,
> Death-hallowed head.

Of this idea, the 'love drink' is in the end merely the consummation; that is, the climax.

2. Tristan's obligation to Mark is such that by no human reasoning can its infringement be justified. Morally considered, justice belongs to Mark.

3. The lovers' union—their fruition—is death. Isolde's final aria in the opera is triumphant, as any true rendering of the *Liebestod* must always be.

Around these three high points Wagner built his three acts. Having made this selection, he could afford to let the other incidents of the legend adapt themselves. As we have seen, the second Isolt promptly disappears. The Morholt—now called Morold—is no longer Isolde's uncle but a former suitor for her hand. Melot, the spying dwarf in the original, is slain by Kurwenal (Gorvenal) for his treachery. The various love trysts—partly in the forest, partly in

Mark's palace, according to the *Estoire*—are reduced to the one love tryst in Wagner's second act.

No printed words can do justice to that blending of action, speech, and music which is so peculiarly Wagnerian. But in closing this chapter, let me recall some of the chief musical and dramatic motifs to show how effectively they reflect the epic background from which they spring.

As the curtain rises on the first act, the audience sees a tentlike space on the foredeck of a ship. Isolde is lying on a couch, her face buried in the cushions; Brangäne (Brangien), holding back a curtain, is gazing over the side of the ship. From above is heard the voice of a sailor, singing a melancholy song about an Irish girl:

> Westwärts schweift der Blick,
> Ostwärts streicht das Schiff,
> Frisch weht der Wind der Heimat zu:
> "Mein irisch Kind, wo weilest Du?"

> Westward sweeps her look,
> Eastward speeds the ship,
> Fresh blows the wind from off the bow:
> "My Irish maid, where lingerest thou?"

This theme, carried in the strings, is henceforth associated with the sea; note that even the meter imitates the movement of waves. When, after reciting to Brangäne the long misery of her young life, Isolde re-

ceives the 'love drink' and, after Tristan has drunk of
it, she snatches the goblet from his hands and drains
it—"for a time only the orchestra speaks, giving out
and fusing motifs 1 and 2" from the *Tristan* prelude.

These are the Sorrow and Magic motifs blended, and
then the Love Potion motif mingled with that of
Death. The last mentioned is, of course, Wagner's
superb creation: "It is made up of B, C, and low D
Sharp, and is thrown out in a strongly colored line by
the bassoons, basses, and bass clarinet." Yet, lest we
forget, it is ultimately grounded on the Old French
couplet:.

> Isolt ma drue, Isolt m'amie!
> En vus ma mort, en vus ma vie.

The lovers now awake to the recognition that each is
eternally the other's, and they pour out their hearts in
rapturous but tragic strains—for they are doomed to
live on into the cruel light of day. The curtain falls as
preparations for landing are going on, the orchestra
"ringing out, in mockery, a vigorous, joyous version
of the sea motif."

The second act begins with the longing for 'freedom.' And the central theme of this act, the *Liebes-
traum*, is both a spiritual and a sensuous awakening.
The motif—No. 26 in the score—is set to the words:

So stürben wir, um ungetrennt:
Ewig, einig, ohne End'.

So would we die, ne'er to sunder,
Forever, united, without end.

This release is granted them as the curtain falls on the last act—too late for King Mark, who is present, to set back the hand of fate. As was remarked above, Wagner retained the arrival of Isolde on the ship from Cornwall. But before she touches the shore of Brittany, Tristan has died in a last, vain effort to see her once more. Then Isolde, over his lifeless form, experiences the *Liebestod*. Finally, there surges through the orchestra, "in the sad, piercing tones of the oboe," the theme of Isolde's Longing and Magic.

This Magic, transported by Wagner into unforgettable music, is that elusive and allusive quality which Arnold refers to in his now classic essay, *The Study of Celtic Literature*. The Irish bards first gave it to the world in epic story, Norman and French trouvères put it into romantic form, the Germans, Norse, Czechs, and Italians copied them—but it remained for Richard Wagner to dramatize the theme and set it to rapturous, triumphant music. In *Tristan und Isolde* he carried out his promise to Liszt: to allow human passion "for once to drink its fill." This done, he let Isolde sink lifeless beside her lover.

Meantime, in England, Swinburne—conscious of his own virtuosity—was to close his *Tristram of Lyonesse* with the static lines:

> And felt his death upon her: and her head
> Bowed, as to reach the spring that slakes all drouth;
> And their four lips became one silent mouth.

Beautiful as this is, it was a far cry from primitive Ireland to Pre-Raphaelite England. But, then, Swinburne was no Wagner.

On Wagner see again Newman's *Life* and his equally reliable *Stories of the Great Operas* (Garden City, n.d.), to which I am greatly indebted for various details, especially as regards the musical motifs of the opera.

On the *aitheda* see the outstanding work of Gertrude Schoepperle, *Tristan and Isolt* (2 vols.; Frankfurt and London, 1913); it is from this work that I take the texts I quote. Lady Gregory's version will be found in *Cuchulain of Muirthemne: The Story of the Red Branch of Ulster* (New York: Scribner's, 1903).

The reference on p. 29 is to the *Disciplina clericalis* of Petrus Alfonsi, and the Latin formula reads: "Ex hac est mihi mors et in hac est mihi vita." It appears to have been Thomas of England who first put it into French.

For further details consult T. P. Cross and C. H. Slover, *Ancient Irish Tales* (New York: Holt, 1936), and Wolfgang Golther, *Tristan und Isolde* (Leipzig: Hirzel, 1907); also Hermann Hagedorn, *Edwin Arlington Robinson: A Biography* (New York: Macmillan, 1938).

III

LANCELOT THE COURTLY LOVER

AS EVERYBODY knows, the love affair of Lancelot is virtually that of Tristan repeated. Lancelot loves Guenevere, as Tristan did Isolt, and Guenevere is Arthur's wife, as Isolt was Mark's; in both cases the hero is disloyal to his king. But here the analogy stops. The responsibility placed on Lancelot as a person, together with the atmosphere surrounding him, is so different from the idea of Tristan that he is landlocked, so to speak, in the Middle Ages and has defied treatment in modern poetry or music— though Tennyson and Morris and Robinson have attempted it.

But his medieval vogue was extraordinary. If you go to the Newberry or the Morgan Library you will find that, among the romances of chivalry there, the *Lancelots* outrank the rest, both in number and in value. The unique 1488 Du Pré edition has the title: "The Last Book of the Round Table, Making Mention of the Deeds and Prowess of My Lord Lancelot of the Lake." But another, long book (now in the British Museum) preceded it, and it is itself made up of three parts: *La tierce partie de Lancelot, La partie du saint graal, La derniere partie de la table ronde.* As Aldous Huxley says: "Every age and class has had its ideal. The ruling class in Greece idealized the magnanimous man. The honnête homme makes his appearance as the ideal of seventeenth century gentlemen; the philosophe as the ideal of their descendents in the eighteenth century. The twentieth has already witnessed the rise and fall of the liberal man and the emergence of the sheeplike social man and the god-like leader. Meanwhile the poor and downtrodden have always dreamed nostalgically of a man ideally well-fed, free, happy, and unoppressed."

Had Huxley added to his list the chivalric man, as the representative of the Middle Ages, he would have named Sir Lancelot; mainly, I think, because Tristan is too heroic, Modred too perverse, Kay too fainthearted, Gawain too sensible, and Perceval too naïve to be typical of that era. Whereas Lancelot, brave and courageous as he is, has inherently something so genteel, so sensitive, so mystical in his makeup as to be characteristic of the twelfth century, from which he cannot without detriment be cut off.

Now, the Middle Ages have an unfortunate name.

Certainly no medieval ever dreamed that he was "medieval" in the derogatory connection we give the word. He was, to be sure, a Christian in a very real and unmodern sense. He accepted with reverence the universe as divinely ordained, and he used his mind or reason to elucidate the process whereby the truth as he saw it (i.e., "revealed truth") could be made clear and intelligible to the mass of men. The essence of that truth was the doctrine of the Incarnation: the belief that God had become man, in the person of Jesus Christ, in order to redeem humanity from the curse of Adam's sin. By his crucifixion, Christ had 'exculpated' Adam and therefore mankind, who were henceforth free to lead useful and thus happy lives.

By and large then to the Middle Ages the first step toward improved social conditions was the recognition of man's sinful state. The sociological implication is evident. How could men be benefited if they were not aware—in the first place—of their evil state, and being aware then seek the means to better it? The Greeks had maintained that evil is 'ignorance' or lack of knowledge. In principle the Middle Ages agreed with them, though there are many ways of defining knowledge. It all depends, and probably always will, on how one conceives of evil in terms of one's primary needs.

But to the scholastic of the twelfth and thirteenth centuries the problem of 'evil' appeared simpler and less complex than to our industrial society today. He consulted his books, and there he found a definite world-order or cosmogony erected on the basis of the Ptolemaic system of astronomy. As the reader will recall, this system went back to the ancients. Its basic idea was that the earth stands at the center of the universe (conceived of as a huge sphere) and that the moon, the sun, the planets, and the fixed stars revolve about the earth—in the shape of successive heavens, outside of which is the Empyrean or tenth heaven, the abode of God and the angels.

In this cosmogony—which, if unscientific (according to present standards), was at least logical—every creature, both real and imaginary, had its proper place, assigned to it in the beginning by God. And the task of the medieval sociologist was to discover how the misfit or maladjustment occurred. As Professor Powicke so convincingly observes: "Christianity was established as an essential element in the social order. Yet it called men to the greatest of adventures; the service and the contemplation of God. It could give excitement to the frivolous; occupation of every kind, physical or intellectual or contemplative, to the serious; and it could offer opportunities in high places as in low to the depraved. It engaged the highest faculties in cooperation with the purpose of God by satisfying their craving for an ordered and just interpretation of life. In the Church human self-esteem was gratified. . . . . Through the Church man could escape from the sense of frustration by dedicating himself to the glory of God."

I might add that, when it came to practical matters, this dedication signified one essential thing; namely, the necessity of bringing the individual into accord with the universe. As we used to say, when referring to the United States, *e pluribus unum*, "out of many one"; we forget that the catholicity of the Middle Ages depended on the assumption that a unity could be effected out of the many, disparate, conflicting human beings with which the earth is filled.

The astonishing thing is that, abstract as all this sounds, it was presented to the medieval schoolboy in a form which he readily understood. For he was grounded in two fundamental subjects which our modern schools tend to neglect: (1) in mathematics, which is the art of thinking logically, and (2) in grammar, which is the art of effective verbal expression. The point I wish to make is the extent—or perhaps one should say, extreme—to which the medieval pedagogue pushed his passion for order. Just as there are seven days in the week, so, he argued, there are seven liberal arts (the trivium and the quadrivium), seven wise men, seven worthies, seven planets—seven this and seven that! So he set up seven Cardinal Virtues and, corresponding to them, seven Deadly Sins. The number was not really important, but the correspondence was; for on this correspondence the divine harmony or balance of the universe appeared to rest.

Now Chivalry, as distinguished from Feudalism (which has to do with landed property), was a social institution based on the relationship of the sexes. Ideally considered, the one sex balanced the other by being its counterpart in social as well as in physical qualities. If woman is true, man will be brave; or, to express the idea in medieval terms, if the knight is active in arms and not slothful, the lady will be loyal to him and chaste in her attitude to others. Geoffrey of Monmouth, in the *Historia regum Britanniae*—the book we dwelt on above—affirms that the ideal was characteristic of the court of King Arthur. He means, of course, before Modred had undermined it, and with justifiable pride he sums up the situation in those innocent times by saying:

> Efficiebantur ergo castae et meliores,
> et milites pro amore illarum probiores.

> Thus [the women] became more chaste and better,
> and the knights for love of them more brave.

A cynic may wonder at this primitivistic touch on the part of Geoffrey; and so probably did his medieval readers. On the whole, however, even the most worldly among them would have agreed that the two brightest virtues are industry and continence, just as their opposites, amid the blackest sins, are sloth (laziness) and lust. The order in which the sins occur varied according to the relative importance that the Church gave them from time to time. But down to Chaucer's day, in the fourteenth century, the order was as follows: pride, envy, wrath, sloth, avarice, gluttony, lust. They go back to the Bible, to I John 2:16, where concupiscence of the flesh, concupiscence of the eyes, and pride or vainglory are condemned.

Now Lancelot of the Lake was never slothful—sloth being a trait reserved for Erec, another Arthurian knight. Least of all was he proud or envious or avaricious. But he was enslaved by Guenevere, and Guenevere was his liege's wife. His dilemma, as I pointed out, is that of Tristan, and it was planned to be so by Chrétien de Troyes, the French poet who invented the Lancelot-Guenevere complex. Indeed, Chrétien wrote a lyric of which the following stanza makes clear the similarity and the difference:

> Onques del brevage ne bui
> Dont Tristans fu enpoisonez,

> Mes plus me fet amer que lui
> Fins cuers et bone volentez.

> Never of the potion did I drink
> Whereby Tristan was poisoned,
> But more than him caused me to love
> A noble heart and a good will!

A gulf separates the two types of lovers. They belong to different worlds. Tristan is bound to Isolt by fate, Lancelot is bound to Guenevere by his own choice. Lancelot knows so well what he is doing that, in his heart, he exults—for his is no blind fury, no madness inflicted on him by destiny; it is the fruition and glory of all that he has worked for in life. Or, to state the case in terms suitable to the twelfth century, Lancelot assumes responsibility for an act for which he knows he will suffer—on account of Guenevere, the wife of Arthur.

This is no *jeu de mots*. Lancelot is far from being precious. Nor is he, like some modern, denying the divine law. He is humbly transgressing the moral law in the expectation that—in the end—he will atone for his transgression. He is an orthodox, medieval Christian, conscious of the fact that the divine order is ineluctable. As Dante, the most gifted of all medieval poets, said:

> E la sua volontate è nostra pace.
> And God's will is our peace.

Let us now turn to the Lancelot legend proper in order to see what its historical development was. Strange to say, a connected account of Lancelot is first met with in Middle High German. In 1194, about a year after Richard Cœur-de-Lion, returning from a crusade, had been taken prisoner by Leopold, Duke of Austria, hostages for his release were sent from England to Vienna, and among them was an Anglo-Norman knight whose name is Hugh de Morville. There is some doubt that he is the same person as the Hugh de Morville notorious for the part he took in the murder of Thomas Becket, Archbishop of Canterbury, in 1170, whom T. S. Eliot has included in his drama *Murder in the Cathedral*. In any case, the Hugh who went to Vienna had a gentler side to his nature, which appears in the fact that he carried to Austria a French work, now lost, on Lancelot. Here is another link between the Angevin rulers of England (for Hugh was a hostage for Richard I) and Arthurian romance, as stated in my first chapter. By channels unknown to us today Hugh de Morville's manuscript passed into the hands of a Swiss priest, Ulrich von Zatzikhoven, who put it into German under the title of *Lanzelet*.

Ulrich keynotes his otherwise disconnected story by calling Lancelot *wîpsaelig*. Literally the word means 'fortunate in women.' Actually it refers to a character trait which the nineteenth-century romantics called "nympholepsy," and we moderns, quite frankly, "sex appeal." Whatever the name, the trait was not opprobrious, and it became as characteristic of Lancelot as wisdom was of Oliver or Gawain and foolhardiness of Kay. Tennyson's weaver of dreams, the Lady of Shalott, meets her fate when her mirror cracks the moment Lancelot's image is reflected in it. And most, if not all, of the episodes in Ulrich's poem are concerned with fair ladies whom Lancelot fatally attracts. Four times in the course of the tale he marries, after killing the lady's oppressor, and each wife—except one only, Iblis—passes noiselessly from the scene and from Lancelot's remembrance, "unwept, unhonoured, and indeed unsung." Imbedded, however, in Ulrich's version, one episode emerges clearly in the thread of the story and forms the background for later romancers. It deals with the hero's abduction and education by the Lady of the Lake, and thus explains why he is later termed "Lancelot of the Lake."

As Ulrich sketches the incident, it runs as follows:

Shortly after the hero's birth, his father, king of Gwynned in Wales (note that again we are on Celtic soil), is attacked and slain. His wife, seeing him fall, rushes to his assistance, but before doing so she lays the infant Lancelot on the ground in the meadow where she was stopping. Here the Lady of the Lake discovers the child and carries him off to her Otherworld kingdom "beneath the waves"—an obvious parallel to the Avalon motif in the Arthur story proper. There she rears him with the design that, when grown to manhood, Lancelot shall kill her enemy, the enchanter Iweret. In carrying out her purpose, the hero not only sets free the Lady of the Lake's own son, Mabuz, whom Iweret has bespelled, but he also wins the hand of the fair Iblis—the one wife whom, according to Ulrich, he does not desert.

Important, in this connection, is the upbringing that the fairy lady gives him. It is of course chivalric. And the emphasis on conduct, that is, 'good manners,' increases as the legend passes from Ulrich's treatment to that of the later story-tellers. But even in Ulrich the fairy godmother knows that her charge has social possibilities and that they will be exercised in the strife of war and love. As a consequence, when he finally leaves her, to re-enter the world of men, she equips him in this manner:

She gave him armour as white as a swan [note the analogue with Lohengrin]—a coat of mail all hung with little golden bells —a shield with an eagle [the noblest of all birds]—and a sword that cut into iron and steel, for it was forged with evil intent.

If the last phrase can be interpreted symbolically, it refers not only to war but also to love, for Lancelot's gaze was fatal to those women upon whom it fell.

From what has been said it is obvious that the German Lanzelet is not yet the Arthurian Lancelot, the lover of Guenevere. But, except for this single devotion, he possesses most of his traits: the mysterious fairy upbringing, the attractiveness to women, the necessary chivalric training. The Arthur saga proper, according to the *Historia regum Britanniae*, lacked such a lover. It is true, Geoffrey had made Modred the abductor of Guenevere and a traitor to Arthur. Even the tragic background had been provided, since Geoffrey uses the figure of Modred to motivate the war against the King and that "last sad battle" at Camlan, in which Arthur fell. But Modred had a base soul, and psychologically he was unfit for further poetic treatment. In short, by 1170 the time was ripe for some great poet to seize upon the Lancelot *Märchen* and, by incorporating it into the Galfridian setting, make it the romantic kernel of the rise and fall of the Round Table. That good fortune was reserved for the French trouvère, Chrétien de Troyes.

On the other hand, Chrétien hardly knew the *Lanzelet* poem, certainly not in its German form. But he may have been acquainted with the story or stories contained in Hugh de Morville's French original. What is still more significant is that he knew life at French and Provençal courts of the twelfth century. His own protectress was the Countess Mary of Champagne, daughter of that wrecker of hearts, Eleanor of Poitou, whose grandfather was the first troubadour poet, William of Aquitaine. During his sojourn at Troyes, Chrétien must have come into contact with courtly life at its best and at its worst. He knew the frailties to which these high-placed ladies were subject. He had seen the sumptuousness—the vair and the gray, the samite and the ermine—with which their bodies were clad. And, with his tongue in his cheek, he had made a mental note of the flash in Mary's or Eleanor's eye as some great champion at arms carried off the prize at a medieval tournament. Besides, historically speaking, he could not have been ignorant of the political reasons that underlay the divorce (in 1152) of Eleanor from Louis VII of France and her sudden marriage to Henry of Anjou, subsequently Henry II of England. It must have been clear to him, as it is to us, that in these surroundings to speak of love and marriage in the same breath was out of the question.

It is no wonder, therefore, that at Mary of Champagne's own bidding Chrétien refashioned the Lance-

lot story into a romance on Lancelot and Guenevere,
which he covertly entitled—after a short incident in
it—*Le Roman de la Charrete*.

In this version of the story Lancelot becomes the
courtly lover par excellence of European literature.

Volumes have been written on 'courtly love.' As a
recognized public institution it could never have existed—though so-called 'courts of love' were doubt-
less held as a social game or pastime. It is easy enough
to define its external traits, though its spiritual or, indeed, moral import is foreign to democratic thinking.
As is well known, courtly love is not conjugal. It is
based on the assumption that love and marriage are
incompatible; for the excellent reason that, in the
feudal twelfth century, marriage had become more and
more of a political affair, since, in territories not subject to the Salic law, property often descended in the
female line, and always, in such cases, the custom pre-
vailed of marrying off women for the bargaining power they possessed. To cite an illustrious example,
known to Chrétien—when Eleanor of Poitou married
Henry II, she carried with her as an inheritance from
her ancestors nearly half of western and southern
France. It is unnecessary to multiply examples. But
any system which made woman the object of political

[handwritten marginalia: not a symbol of eternal devotion]

[handwritten note at bottom: Love can be expressed in different ways, depending upon the society in which one lives]

or economic barter had to make allowances elsewhere for what we call 'human nature.' And this concession feudal society made in granting her a 'lover' who could rarely be her husband.

At the same time, nothing can be further from the truth than the belief that under courtly love sexual promiscuity or license was allowed or even tolerated. The Church of course frowned on adultery; and adulterous and therefore blameworthy in the Church's view as the courtly love affair was, secrecy and fidelity were its law and its only means of escaping censure. In Chrétien's romance Lancelot's single devotion to Guenevere reigns supreme, no matter how attractive he remained to other women. And the charm, as well as the lure, of courtly love was the discretion for which the relationship called. This gave it its aristocratic flavor; the silence as well as the words of the lovers is significant. The one thing that Guenevere studiously avoids—in Arthurian story—is betrayal of Lancelot or herself by speech.

Now the importance of Chrétien's romance today is that it survives in a much-developed prose form, dating at the earliest from the thirteenth century. This is the so-called prose *Lancelot*, or *Grail-Lancelot*, for it contains also the story of the Grail, as in the 1488 incunabulum mentioned above—where pretty much everything Arthurian was welded into one continuous plot on the model of Geoffrey's *Historia*. It was handsomely transcribed and adorned with miniatures. It constituted one of the treasures of the Duc de Berry's library in Paris. And in a somewhat condensed form it came (about 1469) into the hands of Sir Thomas Malory, who paraphrased it in cadenced English prose and gave it the now classic title of the *Morte Darthur*. In this way Lancelot's very name was hid behind the event of which he was ultimately the cause; namely, the death of Arthur. In Italy, however, the name *Galeotto* mentioned by Dante as the book which Paolo and Francesca were reading when they were slain by the tyrant Malatesta refers to the love plot, in its purest and most serious aspect. There the name is taken from Galehaut, the friend in the prose *Lancelot* who manages the first meeting of the lovers, where—with real psychological insight—the author lets Guenevere pretend dissatisfaction with Lancelot in order to veil the impression he has made upon her. A Spanish version of the story was also popular. Thus, through the prose rendering, the legend of Lancelot and Guenevere was disseminated over Europe.

Thanks to the efforts of Lucy A. Paton, the French story is accessible in a modern English rendering. I

quote two passages from it: The first, to mark the in-
terruption of the lovers, after Galehaut had led Lancelot into the Queen's presence; the second, to mark
Lancelot's final renunciation of her:

"Now tell me," said she, "all these exploits that ye have done,
for whom did ye them?"

"Lady, for you."

"What," said she, "love ye me then so well?"

"Lady," said he, "I love not so well myself or another."

"And since when," said she, "have ye loved me so well?"

"Lady," said he, "since I was called knight, and yet I was
not."

"And by the faith that ye owe me, whence came the love that
ye have for me?"

At these words that the Queen spake it befell that the Lady of
Malohaut (who watched them in the meadow where they were
talking) coughed, knowing what she did, and she raised her head
that she had held bowed. He, that had many times heard her,
heard her now, and he looked at her, and he knew her, and he had
such fear and pain in his heart that he might not make answer to
that which the Queen asked of him, and he began to sigh right
heavily. . . . . And the more he looked at the Lady of Malohaut,
the more was his heart at misease. Of this the Queen was ware,
and she saw that he looked piteously toward the ladies and she
checked him.

"Lady," said he, "ye made me love you, ye who made me your
lover if your mouth erred not." . . . .

"I' faith," said the Queen, " 'twas a word spoken in a happy
hour, and God be praised that He led me to speak it. But I took
it more lightly than ye did, and to many a knight have I said it

LANCELOT'S CONFESSION TO THE HERMIT

where I thought of naught beyond the saying. . . . . And your
bearing showeth that ye love I know not which of those ladies
yonder more than ye love me . . . . and ye dare not look at them
directly. So I well perceive that your thoughts are less for me
than ye make semblance that they are. Now by the faith that
ye owe the being that ye most love, tell me which she is?"

The scene is like a miniature drama, so fraught it is
with suspense and so delicately is it managed. How
skilfully the author uses the coughing of the Lady of
Malohaut, just at the right moment. It is a warning.
But it is more than that; it brings the Queen back to
reality. In a different sphere, it is like the "knocking
at the gate" in *Macbeth*. And the Queen, once more
herself, makes her listeners as well as Lancelot think
that she does not believe him! It is obvious that the
Lancelot has gone far beyond the *Tristan* in subtlety
and in characterization. In both respects it is a medieval masterpiece.

On the same high level is Lancelot's confession to
the hermit, near the close of his career:

And Lancelot thought a little, as one that never had disclosed
how it was between him and the Queen. . . . . And ever the good
man admonished him to renounce his sin and utterly leave it be,
for otherwise would he have shame, if he followed not his counsel; and he assured him of eternal life, if he confessed it, and of
perdition, if he concealed it. And by his good words and good
examples he so wrought for him that Lancelot began to speak:

"Sir," said Lancelot, "I am dead in sin for a lady that I have loved all my life, to wit, Queen Guenevere, the wife of King Arthur. She it is that hath given me gold and silver in abundance, and the rich gifts that I have aforetime given to poor knights. She it is that hath set me in full great ease and in the high estate wherein I now am. She it is for love of whom I have done the mighty deeds of arms whereof all the world speaketh. She it is that hath brought me from poverty to riches and from want to all earthly good. But I wot well that for this sin because of her our Lord is so wroth against me that He plainly manifested it to me yestereven.

. . . . *things — in her*

And when he had told him all his estate and all his life, he prayed him before God to give him counsel. *was his*

"Forsooth, sir," said he, "no counsel would avail you aught, if ye promise not God that ye will not again fall into this sin. But if ye will wholly forsake it, and cry unto God for mercy, and repent you with your whole heart, I believe that our Lord will number you with His servants and will open to you the gate of Heaven, where eternal life is prepared for all them that enter therein." *Strength made whole.*

"Sir," said Lancelot, "ye will tell me naught that I shall not do it, if God granteth me life."

"Then I require you," said the good man, "that ye promise me that ye will never offend your Creator in committing mortal sin with the Queen nor any other lady, not in any other way whereby ye would anger Him."

And he promised him as a loyal knight.

The end of the story is a foregone conclusion. Through this sin the Arthurian order is doomed—just as in the Germanic saga 'greed,' symbolized by the

Hoard of the Nibelungs, is the undoing of the Volsungs. When all the characters in the story (Arthur, Gawain, Kay, Sagremor, and Guenevere) have died, Lancelot lives on attended only by his faithful companion, Sir Bors. When finally he closes his eyes on a world that has long ago forsaken him, he has been shriven and absolved of the seventh deadly sin in the medieval hierarchy, that of 'lust.' It is to lead up to this conclusion that the Lancelot story was composed in its prose form, and therefore it is medieval. For without this last step—that of salvation—the story, according to medieval terms, would have been incomplete, and, what is more important, it would have had no significance in the Christian world-order. Seeking the peace that passeth understanding, Lancelot at the end sees the light—the light of redemption.

It is singular, but of all modern poets who have treated the Lancelot theme only Robinson—and as should be, for entirely personal reasons—has immortalized this particular moment:

> He turned
> Again; and he rode on, under the stars,
> Out of the world, into he knew not what,
> Until a vision chilled him and he saw,
> Now as in Camelot, long ago in the garden,
> The face of Galahad who had seen and died,
> And was alive, now in a mist of gold.

> He rode on into the dark, under the stars,
> And there were no more faces. There was nothing.
> But always in the darkness he rode on,
> Alone; and in the darkness came the light.

The general reader will get all he needs from Lucy Allen Paton, *Sir Lancelot of the Lake: A French Prose Romance of the Thirteenth Century* (New York: Harcourt, 1929). The volume is provided with an excellent introduction and notes.

For historical details see also James Douglas Bruce, *Evolution of Arthurian Romance* (2d ed.; Baltimore: Johns Hopkins Press, 1928).

Ptolemy's great work went under the name of *Almagest*, derived from the Arabic translation of the Greek text made about A.D. 827. It was put into medieval Latin by Gerard of Cremona and is mentioned by Chaucer in the *Miller's Tale*.

IV

PERCEVAL AND THE GOOD FRIDAY MAGIC

I T IS odd that the Perceval story with its long history, deeply rooted in folk tradition, is familiar today mainly through Wagner's music-drama *Parsifal*. That is true even on European soil, where the tale of the Great Fool (the *Dümmlingsmärchen*), the ancestor of Perceval, is indigenous. In the Scottish "Lay of the Great Fool" he is still called by his Gaelic name, Amadán Mor; and the boyhood exploits of Finn mac Cumhail, hero of the Irish Ossianic cycle, have similarities with the adventures of the youthful Perceval. The story rests upon two axes: the fact that the hero is a simpleton (Wagner calls him "der reine Thor") and the manner in which he is made 'wise,' either, as in the Finn cycle, by eating the meat of a magic salmon or, as in the sophisticated versions, by being stirred by pity for those whom he has ignorantly wronged. Whoever has heard the opera *Parsifal* is acquainted with its dominant motif: "Durch Mitleid

59

wissend, der reine Thor''—''Moved by pity, the pure fool.''

But Wagner was indebted for his knowledge of the story to the medieval *Parzival*, a poem of Wolfram von Eschenbach, who in turn took the thread of his plot from the *Perceval le Galois* or *Conte del graal* by Chrétien de Troyes. In retelling the folk tale for his twelfth-century public Chrétien clothed it in feudal, Arthurian costume. He incorporated with it an account of a mysterious dish, the so-called *Graal* or Grail. And he made the whole into a romantic novel with a religious educational flavor.

The boy's mother—Chrétien tells us at the outset—fears that her child will be killed by his father's enemies in a tournament. This had been her husband's fate, and to save her son from a similar end she carries him off to the solitude of a forest, far from the world of fighting men. There he is reared in ignorance of knighthood and develops into a simpleton; so naïve and uncouth that people actually take him for a Welshman, the title *Perceval le Galois* (i.e., 'the Welshman') being a dig at the uncouth habits of the Welsh people.

The inevitable happens. One day the youth strays upon some knights who have lost their way in the forest. Because of their glistening armor he takes them

THE HOLY GRAIL AT PENTECOST

"Clothed in white semite, mystic, wonderful"

for angels, and innocently he kneels down to worship them. Rebuffed for his stupidity, he upbraids his mother for deceiving him—until, heartbroken, the good woman is compelled to let him go forth into the world. But before he leaves her, she gives him definite moral instructions (the kind a mother would give), which again he follows to the letter and thus involves himself in trouble.

Arriving at the court of King Arthur, he brashly rides into the dining-hall on horseback; awkwardly knocks off Arthur's headgear; and, being scolded by Sir Kay for his boorishness, says that he will not accept knighthood from Arthur unless he can be a red knight. Then begin his real adventures. The first is his victory over the Red Knight, whom, like David, he slays in an unconventional and unchivalric manner (by hurling a javelin through his eye), and whom he then attempts to dispossess of his armor by building a fire under his body. Another adventure is his rescue of a beleagured lady, Blanchefleur, the recollection of whose beauty (she has an Irish 'love spot' on her cheek) becomes his obsession. And a third, important adventure is his meeting with a wise old man, Gornemanz, who, aware of the lad's native ability, undertakes to give him instruction in the fundamental rules and obligations of chivalry.

This is one of the earliest recorded passages regarding the Order of Chivalry. Moreover, it constitutes a turning-point in Perceval's career. The rule on which Gornemanz lays most stress, in his definition of chivalry, is that young people must not ask foolish questions. The Bible, as he points out to Perceval, teaches (Prov. 10:19) that "he who curbs his speech is a wise man." As a social maxim, nothing could be sounder. The trouble is that a simpleton will take the rule literally and refrain from speaking when a question, wisely put, would solve a difficulty. As Molière was to observe centuries later: "A wise man who remains silent is no better than a fool who never opens his mouth." And Perceval is still the fool, as the story proceeds to show.

Perceval has left "Beaurepaire," Blanchefleur's castle. He has ridden hard all day, night is approaching, the country around him is barren and deserted, and he himself weary and dejected, when quite by chance he sees upon a river a skiff and in it an old man who is fishing. The fisherman is infirm and unable to walk; but he directs the youth to his own castle (beyond or in a mountain), in which, though it is difficult to find, Perceval is sumptuously received.

This mysterious person is the Fisher King. Wagner, taking his cue from Wolfram (his medieval source),

calls him Amfortas. Him Perceval is to cure; but, if he
is to do so, he must ask a certain question, the nature
of which recalls one of those unspelling formulas
known to folklore, like the "Open sesame" of the
Arabian Nights or the riddle which in ancient times
Oedipus solved and thus destroyed the Sphinx. But
will Perceval ask it? Has he—who deserted his mother
—the compassion for the Fisher King's suffering which
will make him speak out, against Gornemanz' teaching? This is the dramatic crux of the whole story.
And the episode in which it is found is known as "The
Unasked Question," a part of which I shall quote
from Newell's admirable English paraphrase:

The hall (of the castle) was as wide as it was long; in the center, on a bed, lay a nobleman (the Fisher King) whose hair was
blent with gray; his cap was made of sable, lined with purple
cloth, and his robe of the same stuff. He reclined, leaning on his
elbow; in front between four columns of bronze, which supported
the firedog, burned a huge fire; four hundred men could have found
room about the fireplace. Standing on either side, the servants
brought Perceval before the king, who greeted him saying:
"Friend, be not vexed that I rise not to greet you." He answered:
"Sir, in God's name, no more; be assured, it disturbeth me not."
The lord raised himself as well as he could, and said: "Friend,
come hither, and seat yourself at my right hand."

.   .   .   .

The hall was lit with many candles; while they spake of this
and that, a varlet entered who bore a lance which he held by the
middle; he passed between the fire and the bed, so that those who

were seated saw the lance, with its glistening blade; from the point of it flowed a drop of blood that coursed to the bearer's hand. The visitor saw the marvel, and wondered what it meant; but he bethought him of the teacher who had warned him not to be free of speech; he feared, if he spake, that it would seem rude; therefore he asked no question.

Presently came two fair youths, with candlesticks of chiselled gold, each having ten candles or more. They were accompanied by a damsel, who with both hands carried a dish (the *grail*)—it emitted such lustre that the candles lost their light, like the stars when the sun or moon rises. After her went a second maid, bearing a silver trencher. The grail was covered with jewels, the richest in the world. Like the bearer of the lance, this company passed in front of the couch, from chamber to chamber; the youth saw and dared not ask 'whom they served with the grail'; yet he feared to be wrong, for he remembered to have heard that one may err by keeping silent too long as well as by speaking overmuch; howbeit, he put no question.

When the host bade, were brought water and towels; the master and his guest laved their hands in the warm water. Two servants brought an ivory table and set it before them; while two others followed, each carrying a trestle of ebony, a wood which never decays; on the trestles they set the table, which was covered with a cloth as white as any ever used by cardinal or pope. The first course was a haunch of fat venison, seasoned with pepper; clarets were served in golden goblets, while a varlet carved the venison, laying the slices on the silver trencher. Meantime, the grail passed again before their eyes. . . . . Perceval knew not to whom it was carried, though he longed to know; he said to himself that on the morrow, ere he took leave, he would ask one of the varlets of the house. So the matter was deferred [he asked no question].

On the morrow, of course, Perceval finds the place deserted:

> He called and knocked, but there was no reply; he turned to the door of the hall, found it open, and descended the stair; he found his horse saddled, while his lance and shield were leaning against the wall. He mounted his horse and gazed about, but could perceive no servant, no varlet, no squire; he rode to the castle gate and found the drawbridge lowered. He thought that the household must have gone to the forest, to hunt stags and roes, and said to himself that he would ride after, to inquire why the lance bled and whither was carried the grail. He issued from the gate; as he came to the foot of the bridge, he felt his horse's feet rise, the steed made a bound, or both horse and man would have been hurt. He turned and saw that the bridge had been raised. "Ha," he cried, "thou who hast lifted the bridge, come forth, that I may look on thee, and ask a thing that I desire to know." The words were wasted; there was no reply.

Apart from the significance of this scene, as a cult or ceremonial, is its great artistic value. Of that there can be only one opinion. Three times the theme rises to a head, and each time it is shattered against Perceval's stubborn hesitation, so that when finally he is ready to ask there is nobody to reply. Herewith end the "boyhood exploits" of the hero—what the Irish in the case of Finn or Cuchulinn would have called his *echtra*. What follows is necessarily his punishment and despair and, finally, his redemption or awakening from error. In Perceval's case, through pity.

But, before resuming the narrative, let us consider for a moment the Fisher King and the ceremonial of which he is the object. The 'fish' is a recurrent symbol of eternal life. It is found in temples and shrines the world over. An early Christian mystical symbol was the word IChThUS, or 'fish,' where the capital letters stood for the initials of the Greek words for 'Jesus Christ,' 'Son of God,' 'Savior.' There is also a vague suggestion in the Bleeding Lance and in the Grail (about which the hero is to ask) of the lance of the Crucifixion and the dish or even chalice of the Last Supper. But how did these orthodox elements get into the Great Fool story? And how explain the Fisher King's wound, which is not, like Christ's, in his side but, as Chrétien implies and Wolfram baldly says, in his generative parts? The answer is obvious. Whatever Christian coloring the French romance may have taken on, originally the Fisher King was a symbol of reproductive Nature. And, if there be any doubt as to what he represents, one need only recall the roll of Osiris in Egypt, Tammuz in Assyria, Eshmun in Phoenicia, or Dionysus or Adonis among the Greeks. They, too, had a corresponding disability, and the rites connected with them are concerned with a cult in which a neophyte, like Perceval, has a share. Moreover, thus considered, the food-giving dish or

Grail, about which we shall have more to say in the next chapter, appears functionally in its logical place. It also is primarily a symbol of productivity, and whether it contains originally the body of the slain God (as in the Christian Eucharist) or is chiefly a magic source of refreshment, like the German *Tischchen-deck-dich*—that is a matter of no great consequence here. Indeed, Chrétien's imitator, Wolfram, endows the Grail with both functions. It is supplied by Heaven with a holy wafer, a sort of 'host':

> Ein tûb von himel swinget:
> Ûf den stein diu bringet
> Ein kleine wîze oblât.

> A dove swings down from heaven,
> It brings the grail a leaven:
> A wafer small and white.

And it furnishes Arthurian knights with whatever food they may desire:

> Swâ nâch jener bot die hand;
> Daz er al bereite vant,
> Spîse warm, spîse kalt,
> Spîse niwe unt dar zuo alt,
> Daz zam unt daz wilde.

> Whereto anyone stretched his hand out,
> That he discovered all about:
> Dishes warm and dishes cold,
> Dishes new and dishes old,
> Domestic food and wild game.

The medieval story-tellers were eclectic. They did not scrutinize too closely their sources. Anything was grist for their Christianizing dialectic. But the scene they were depicting was a nature ritual or cult, the success of which depended on the moral fitness of the initiate. This is clear from the Fisher King, the Grail, the Unasked Question—Perceval's whole experience at the castle—and this theme they combined with the folk tale about the Great Fool.

But let us return to the hero's subsequent adventures. The curse now falls upon Perceval. Arthur finds him and brings him back to his court. There he is denounced by the Fisher King's emissary, the Loathly Damsel. Out of her Wagner was to create the sinister figure of Kundry the Temptress—an amalgam of all that Wagner felt at the time with regard to *das Ewigweibliche*. In Chrétien, however, her chief function is to render the hero mad:

Her black hair was tressed with two braids . . . . iron-dark were her hands and nails, and her closed eyes small, like a rat's; her nose was of ape and cat, and her lips of ass and bull; her red teeth resembled the marrow of an egg; bearded was she, humped breast and back, her loins and shoulders twisted, like the roots of a tree. Never in royal court was such a damsel seen.

She hurls her imprecation at the hero's head:

"Unhappy is he who waiteth a time, when occasion offers! Wretched wert thou, who hadst time and place and leisure enough. To thy grief wert thou mute. Hadst thou asked, the king who despairs would have been healed of his wounds, and in peace retained his land, which now he will never possess."

"Knowest thou what will happen because of thy fault?"

"Women will lose their husbands, lands will be laid waste, maidens will remain without counsel—orphaned and widowed will they be, and many knights perish. All their sorrows will befall on thy account!"

Then she proclaims a series of quests—to Montesclaire with its Sword of the Strange Hangings; to Castle Orguellous where abide, each with his ladylove, five hundred and sixty six heroes! Arthur's knights are in a turmoil at the thought of so much adventure. But Perceval, stricken down, makes a solemn vow:

No two nights will he lie in the same hostel, nor shun any dangerous pass of which he may hear, nor avoid encountering the bravest of knights or two at the same time, until he learns who was served with the grail, and . . . . discovered why the lance bled—this quest would he not abandon by reason of any woe.

The result is that for five long years he roams the forest, like a hounded beast, distraught and aimless. He forgets all human obligations, except one: a vague recollection that he must return to his forsaken mother. Torn now this way, now that—unkempt, unwashed, never doffing his armor—he strays upon some knights and ladies in penetential garb, and they remind him, who has lost all sense of time, that he is wearing his armor on Good Friday, the day on which his Savior died for mankind on the cross.

Then follows his confession to a hermit—his own uncle. Shriving him of his sin, the good man informs him:

> A sin hath harmed thee of which thou knowest naught; the grief of thy mother, when thou didst desert her, so that swooning on the earth she lay . . . . before the gate of her manor, and of that sorrow she died.
>
> Because of this sin . . . . naught didst thou ask concerning the lance or the grail; therefore hath much evil befallen thee. . . . . Sin closed thy lips, when thou didst gaze on the iron that never yet was staunched, and ask not why it bled; foolish wert thou, when thou didst fail to learn who was served with the grail.
>
> My brother is he, thy mother his sister and mine. Of the Rich Fisher I know that he is son of the king who lets himself be served by the grail. . . . .
>
> So holy a thing is the grail, and so spiritual is he that for his sustenance he needeth no more than the wafer which is brought in the grail. Twenty years hath he spent in such state that never hath he been able to issue from the chamber, whither thou sawest the grail carried.
>
> Now I enjoin thee and grant thee penance of thy sin.

Books have their fates. In this case death prevented Chrétien from completing his romance, though a score of others—including Wolfram—not only finished it but wrote sequels to it. Welsh literature has a version, the *Peredur ab Evrawc*, in which there is no Grail, no sacred vessel, but only the lance and a detruncated head on a platter to remind the hero that he must take vengeance. How Chrétien would have ended his story no one knows, though judging by its motivation that seems clear enough: Perceval returns to the castle, asks the fateful question, thus curing the Fisher King and benefiting his land and its inhabitants, and finally succeeds him.

In one respect Chrétien's moralizing habit, which is accountable for the Good Friday episode, was unfortunate. As a story based on the theme of the Great Fool, it would have been better narrative to let the hero himself see the light and then return, of his own will, to solve the riddle. This is the 'awakening,' the *anagnoresis*, as the Greeks say, that one would be led to expect. But, living in clerical surroundings, the medieval trouvère gave the story a slant from which, ironically, it has never recovered. As it is—and to this our next chapter is devoted—the recognition motif does not disappear, but the thirteenth century makes it over into a purely mystical experience in which the virginal Galahad effaces the far too human Perceval. Thus one hero replaces another. As for modern authors, Tennyson still mentions Sir Percivale. But the latter is a pale reflection of his medieval ancestor. Won to holy orders and bereft of worldly appeal, he remarks pensively:

> Lo, if I find the Holy Grail itself
> And touch it, it will crumble into dust.

This character is aeons removed from the strong-willed, stubborn, headstrong lad known to early medieval literature.

Again it is Wagner to whom the modern world is indebted for rescuing the Perceval theme from oblivion, quite aside, on the one hand, from the defeatist Schopenhauer strain of which he made it the vehicle and, on the other, from the inspiring music in which he clothed it. For this we have to thank—at least in part—his knowledge of Wolfram von Eschenbach's classic, the Middle High German *Parzival*.

The idea of an opera on Parsifal had taken firm hold of Wagner's mind about 1859, during his sojourn in Venice, soon after the *Tristan* episode began to abate in his turbulent soul. He reports that a magical Good Friday calm had possessed itself of him. "Silent and tranquil," he writes, "I am carried down the grave, melancholy Canal . . . . not a sound anywhere but the gentle gliding·of the gondola and the plashing of the oar. The moon casts broad shadows. I disembark at the steps of my dumb palace. Wide halls and space, inhabited by me alone. My lamp is burning: I take up my book, read a little, muse a good deal. All is still."

How strikingly this scene reminds us of the far-off, mysterious palace of the Fisher King, where Perceval, riding out over the drawbridge, got no answer. More important, however, for the moment is Wagner's own mood. Writing to Frau Wesendonk, he explains that now "he is full of pity and sympathy, less for individuals than for humanity itself, doomed to suffering by the very law of its being: this feeling, he says, is more profound for lower natures than for higher . . . . more profound again for beasts than for men, for the beast's suffering is just dull, hopeless pain, without possibility of redemption from it by the philosophic imagination." Technically Wagner was no philosopher, but he had read the ideas of Schopenhauer and mingled or confused them in his mind with a belief in a Buddhistic Nirvana, in which human beings forgive and—alas!—forget. All this, he reminds Frau Wesendonk, will be made clear some day in the Good Friday scene in *Parsifal*.

The opera was first performed at Bayreuth in July of 1882—nearly twenty-five years later. Meantime, he had dealt with the Grail theme in *Lohengrin* (1850) in a series of motifs that Liszt described as "vaporous ether gradually unfolding itself." This idealism pervades the description Lohengrin gives to Else on their fatal wedding night:

> In fernem Land, unnahrbar euren Schritten,
> Liegt eine Burg, die Monsalvat genannt;
> Ein lichter Tempel stehet dort in Mitten,
> So kostbar, wie auf Erden nichts bekannt:
> Drin ein Gefäss, von wunderthät'gem Segen
> Wird dort als höchstes Heiligtum bewacht—
>
> .   .   .   .
>
> Es heisst der Gral, und selig reinster Glaube
> Ertheilt durch ihn sich seiner Ritterschaft.

> In distant lands, untrod by human steps,
> A castle lies, whose name is Monsalvat,
> And, in its midst, a temple deftly wrought,
> So precious that on earth its equal nowhere is.
> There we do keep a wonder-making dish,
> And guard it as a blessed talisman:
>
> .   .   .   .
>
> It's named the Grail, and holy, purest faith
> Is spread by it throughout our brotherhood.

But, while the atmosphere in *Parsifal* is heavier—freighted, as it seems, with desire—the work in its strange way is a masterpiece.

In opposition to the guileless Perceval, now called Parsifal, Wagner put the sensuous, demonic Kundry, the suggestion for whose character he took from Wolfram, who had thus named the Loathly Damsel of his French source:

> Sie hiez Cundrîe:
> Surziere was ir zuoname.

She was hight Kundry:
Sorceress was her surname.

To this appellation Wagner gave a fresh interpretation. The story now becomes the vehicle of German
messianic ideals—in the manner of Schopenhauer. Already with Fichte and Schelling the thinking 'reason'
(the *noumenon*, as they termed it) was merging into
the world of 'sense' (the *phenomenon*), and man's ob-
jective and subjective functions were losing their en-
tities in the absolute. "He who has once grasped,"
said Schopenhauer, "this identity of all beings, no
longer distinguishes between himself and others; he
partakes of their joys as his own joys, of their suffering
as his own suffering; through compassion the whole
world is made one." We recognize at once the totali-
tarian fallacy, one of the greatest errors of the nineteenth century and surviving into the present. And we
understand Nietzsche's break with Wagner.

At all events, the gulf between Wagner and Chrétien
is now unbridgeable. In the former, reason and sense
are confounded; in the latter, sense had always been
under the control of the reason—no Frenchman would
think otherwise. Even Tennyson, when later he
philosophizes about his own *Idylls*, manages somehow
to let reason war with sense.

To embody his idea, Wagner created the personage

of Kundry. She is to the Grail knight what the Venus of the Hörselberg had been to Tannhäuser. Only her character is more complex, and to make this clear Wagner wove the following story about her career: When Christ was nailed to the cross, Kundry—who was present—laughed at the Savior. His glance, however, had come to rest upon her, and from that moment she had roamed the earth as one possessed (a female Ahasver). In the opera, Kundry is in the power of the enchanter Klingsor. For him she seduces knights on the quest of the Grail. She herself is doomed to live until the innocence of a pure lover— the *reiner Thor*—shall redeem her. This person, of course, is Parsifal. Her satanism consists in the fact that she longs for the good but is forced to do evil.

If now we couple to this motif that of Amfortas, whose suffering she has caused, and the motif of the Holy Grail (designated as No. 2 in the score of the Prelude to the opera) together with the central motif or theme—*Durch Mitleid wissend* (No. 5)—we have the main elements for the three acts of *Parsifal*.

Act I carries us into the landscape of the Grail Castle. The plot of the act culminates in Parsifal's being brought into the presence of the holy vessel now identified with the cup of the Last Supper and the receptacle of Christ's blood—a change from the pagan dish

of Chrétien which was inevitable—and the failure of
the simpleton hero to grasp the meaning of the scene.
As he is then thrust out of the Grail Castle into the
night, a single alto voice carries the theme of *Durch
Mitleid wissend*, other voices from above, that of the
Grail, the bells of the castle peal forth, and the curtain falls on a scene of majesty and pathos interwoven.

Act II, then, centers on Kundry and the curse. The
setting is laid at Klingsor's castle. As the temptress
lures the hero on and he is about to sink into her arms,
he awakens—the 'recognition'—to the remembrance
of his mother and to Amfortas' wound, and he rejects
her. Musically, the act opens with an impetuous introduction, a mingling of the Klingsor motif and that
of Kundry's laughter. It closes on the contrast between the collapse of Klingsor's garden and the liberation of Kundry, who, lifting herself from the ground,
gazes wistfully after Parsifal.

Finally, Act III returns us to a landscape near the
Grail Castle. It is springtime, and the background is
filled with flowers. We see a hermit's hut, where
Kundry announces to Gurnemanz the approach of a
knight in black armor. After the confession—it is
Good Friday—the hero is led off to the Grail Castle.
Motif No. 27 marks the beginning of the now famous
Good Friday magic. Arrived before the Grail, Parsi-

fal is in possession of the spear that Klingsor had hurled at him (symbolizing the lance that had pierced the side of Christ); with it he touches Amfortas' wound, and the cure is achieved. Kundry, gazing at Parsifal, sinks lifeless to the ground, Amfortas and Gurnemanz kneel before Parsifal, who then waves the Holy Grail in blessing over the assembled brotherhood of knights. The opera ends with the mystical strains of the Faith motif (No. 3), the Grail theme (No. 2), and that of the Love Feast (No. 1).

Looking back over this evolution, we note that the Good Friday confession—or, as Wagner phrased it, the Good Friday magic—occupies in the opera a different place from what it did in Chrétien's story. It no longer precedes the 'recognition'—but follows it as a sign of forgiveness and grace. That is what it came to mean in Wagner's personal experience. It was the new life, the renewal or revival of Nature—to which corresponded the peace that had come into Wagner's soul after the Wesendonk episode. Into the composition of this theme went his noblest poetic effort. And the words in which he set it are among the finest in modern poetry. It is Parsifal singing:

> Wie dünkt mich doch die Aue heut' so schön!
> Wohl traf ich Wunderblumen an,
> Die bis zum Haupte süchtig mich umrankten.

How lovely seem the fields to me today!
Did I not find so many wondrous flowers
With stems that luscious grew about my head;

to which Gurnemanz (the hermit uncle) answers:

Nun freut sich alle Kreatur
Auf des Erlösers holder Spur,
Will ihr Gebet ihm weihen.

Rejoicing, each created thing
To the Redeemer's feet does bring
Its prayers as an offering.

Story motifs are pertinacious. In the legend of Perceval there has been always, since the time of Chrétien, a hidden nature ceremonial. It shines through the story in various details: the burning of the Red Knight out of his armor (for that is a way of destroying unfriendly spirits); the curse of the Loathly Damsel, her own appearance, and the barrenness she predicts; the fishing of the King and the nature of his illness. To all this Wagner's Good Friday magic is the fitting climax.

On the Perceval story and the Grail see Bruce, *Evolution*. The passages I quote (with some adaptation) are taken from William Wells Newell, *King Arthur and the Round Table* (2 vols.; Boston and New York: Houghton Mifflin, 1898).

On the Wagnerian sections see, once more, the works, cited above, by Newman; and the chapter on Wagner in Thomas Mann, *Freud, Goethe, Wagner* (New York: Knopf, 1937).

V

THE WASTE LAND AND THE
MYSTICAL GRAIL

THE *Waste Land*, as my readers know, is the title of a now famous poem by T. S. Eliot. It is not a reference to the Dust Bowl of Oklahoma or to the Bad Lands of the Dakotas, although it might well refer to both of them. Eliot first published his poem, as a post-war product, in 1922, and in it he incorporated the following striking passage:

> What are the roots that clutch, what branches grow
> Out of this stony rubbish? Son of man,
> You cannot say, or guess, for you know only
> A heap of broken images, where the sun beats,
> And the dead tree gives no shelter, the cricket no relief,
> And the dry stones no sound of water. Only
> There is shadow under this red rock
> (Come in under the shadow of this red rock)
> And I will show you something different from either
> Your shadow at morning standing beside you
> Or your shadow at evening rising to meet you;
> I will show you fear in a handful of dust.

Then comes, in Eliot's poem, the sailor's song from Wagner's *Tristan*, but split in two and between the parts this image:

'You gave me hyacinths first a year ago;
They called me the hyacinth girl.
—Yet when we came back, late, from the hyacinth garden,
Your arms full, and your hair wet, I could not
Speak, and my eyes failed, I was neither
Living nor dead, and I knew nothing,
Looking into the heart of light, the silence.'
Öd' und leer das Meer.

My reason for quoting this selection is not so much to stress Eliot's poetic method—the method of orchestrating in verse the broken images of life—as to call attention to the central idea of the Waste Land about which his disparate thoughts are grouped. In the "Notes" at the end of the poem Eliot informs the reader that "not only the title, but the plan and a good deal of the symbolism of the poem" were suggested to him by Miss Weston's book on the Grail legend (*From Ritual to Romance*). Thus we are on familiar ground and dealing with a consecrated medieval theme.

As was said in the last chapter, Perceval is already a "culture" hero; that is, his acts have a ritualistic bearing—as cause and effect—in that the fruitfulness of the land and its creatures is dependent on the hero's

behavior. Now, modern scholarship is wary of culture heroes: they are elusive and hard to prove from
the written documents that have come down to us.
But scholars are often unimaginative, and many of
them have failed to observe that when, in Chrétien's
poem, Perceval is expected to heal the Fisher King's
wound—by whatever device the poet chooses to eu-
phemize the idea, he is leading us back to "the earliest
and most primitive of our picture-dreamings," to
Adonis whom the boar slew, to Osiris whose limbs
and organs must be fished out of the Nile, to any one
of the European vegetation gods. Quite specific is the
reference to the 'blighted land' in one of Chrétien's
continuators: here the country goes to waste under
the effect of the spell, but after the 'question' is asked,
the waters flow again, the woods regain their verdure,
and people are blessed in their activities. Eliot's figure of the Phoenician sailor Phlebas, to whom he refers in the verses:

> Gentile or Jew,
> O you who turn the wheel and look to windward,
> Consider Phlebas, who was once handsome and tall as you.

—is but another 'broken image' of this eternal myth.
   When we come to think of it, any population living
close to the soil will in time produce a nature myth of
this general type. In the twelfth and thirteenth cen-

turies France and England were still predominantly
agricultural nations, and their native beliefs inevita-
bly were concerned with the production or failure of
crops. If autumn was to them a dying god, followed
by the blight or waste land of winter, spring was always a resuscitated god whose fruitfulness kept them
alive. How easy it was for the Christian church—
once she became concerned—to reconcile so simple and
natural a rotation with the parallel birth, death, and
resurrection of Christ. Did not Jesus himself use the
homely parables of the Sower and the Mustard Seed
to win converts?

But if the Perceval story was fit for a complete
Christianization—and that was the work of the thirteenth century—it was Chrétien himself who had prepared the way for it by his treatment of the Good Friday confession. Here was the opportunity that the
cleric in Chrétien seized upon. Perceval's sin was
'pride'—his stubbornness had so far misled him that
he had ignored the day on which Christ died; and the
lesson the hermit teaches him is 'humility'—a con-
siderate compassion for others, for his mother, and for
the disabled Fisher King. Out of this theme, interpreted diversely according to Cluniac and Cistercian
teaching, arose two of the greatest Grail works of

the Middle Ages: the *Perlesvaus* and the *Queste del saint Graal*.

It is to these works, both in prose and both the product of great medieval monasteries, that we now turn our attention.

The first of these romances, the *Perlesvaus*, is the product of Glastonbury Abbey. Situated in Somersetshire, south of the Bristol Channel, Glastonbury lies on the river Brue, which in the flood season of the year makes of it an island. Thus it came early to be identified with the Celtic Avalon, both as a place fruitful in 'apples' and as an actual island. Indeed, the well-known lines of Tennyson, quoted in our first chapter, are descriptive of Glastonbury:

> Deep-meadow'd, happy, fair with orchard-lawns
> And bowery hollows crown'd with summer sea.

Founded by the Benedictine order, the Abbey was during the twelfth century the object of skilful propaganda. Its abbot was Henry of Winchester, cousin to King Henry II and favorable to the Angevin cause in its contest with Thomas Becket, Archbishop of Canterbury. So that, after the murder of Becket in 1170, the monks of the monastery set up the claim—false to be sure—that Glastonbury was the primate church of Britain (*fons et origo totius religionis Britanniae*). And, in order to cement the ties between the Abbey and the

ARTHUR'S TOMB AT GLASTONBURY

"Fyrst, ye may see his sepulture in the monasterye of Glastyngburye" (Caxton, *Morte Darthur*, Preface).

crown, they fantastically affirmed that they had discovered the bodies of King Arthur and Guenevere. In fact, in 1191, after the accession of Richard I, that monarch witnessed at Glastonbury the exhumation of the supposed remains of Arthur and his queen and their interment in the Lady Chapel of the monastery, which thus became a national shrine of the races united under the British realm. The support derived for this idea from the *Historia* of Geoffrey of Monmouth (as outlined in our first chapter) is of course obvious. Arthur himself might not come again to rule the British people, but his descendants would— provided they traced their ancestry to the royal tombs in the Abbey.

Against this background, with the purpose of exploiting it piously, the Glastonbury monk composed the *Perlesvaus*.

It is an amazing literary composition. In an allegory of militant Christianity, the author expected his reader to penetrate the shell of chivalric and folklore motifs, based largely on the work of Chrétien and his continuators, to the hidden religious and theological symbolism he desired to portray. Out of Perceval the simpleton, innocent as to life, he made Perlesvaus champion of the faith, innocent as to sin. To emphasize the idea, he even puns on his name: Perlesvaus is the youth who "loses the valleys (where his father lived)," so his name means *Perd les vaux*, but in their place he wins the world for Christ, so his name also means *Par lui fet*, that is, "made by himself." King Arthur himself combats the heathen Welsh and Scotch and, having fallen into sloth, becomes again an active monarch after having witnessed the Christian miracle of transubstantiation. The Fisher King now called Messiah is likened to Christ, and the Grail—originally a food-giving dish—is definitely identified with the receptacle of the Holy Blood and the chalice of the Eucharist.

But the basic theme of the *Perlesvaus* is the Waste Land motif. That is the author's point of departure. Had the hero—in Chrétien's poem—asked the question, all might have gone well with the world. Whereas, owing to his failure, "there happened such great misfortune to Great Britain that all of the islands and all of the lands fell thereby into great suffering." The theme runs through the work like a black thread. Morally it affects most of the characters; beside Arthur and Perlesvaus, Gawain and Lancelot—who seek the Grail vainly. And linked to it closely, as the instruments of evil, are a multitude of Red Knights. In this respect, as in several others, the Glastonbury monk is pillaging his Celtic background. He knew of these 'red creatures' as the demons the folk feared most, as the destroyers of their vegetation and crops—and he allegorized them into enemies of Christianity and hence of Perlesvaus. But in Ireland—which was not far off from Glastonbury—the red horsemen had long before attained literary expression. The classic passage on them is found in the Old Irish *Togail Bruidne Dá Derga* ("The Destruction of Da Derga's Palace"), and it runs as follows:

> When Conaire . . . . was journeying along the road of Cuálu, he marked before him three horsemen (riding) toward the house. Three red frocks had they, and three red mantles: three red bucklers they bore, and three red spears were in their hands: three red steeds they bestrode, and their red heads of hair were on them. Red they were all, both body and hair and raiment, both steeds and men.
>
> Conaire went after them, and overtook them not; but one of the three men answered and said:
>
> "Lo, my son, great news. Weary are the steeds we ride. We ride the steeds of Donn Tetscorach from the elfmounds. Though we are alive, we are dead. Great are the signs; destruction of life: sating of ravens: feeding of crows, strife of slaughter: wetting of sword-edge, shield broken bosses in hours after sundown. Lo, my son!"

The earth-born strength of this description is of course foreign to the Glastonbury monk. Besides, his purpose was to let his hero triumph over all disruptive powers: by the innate force of his Christianity. But the monk knew the folk motif, and he contrasts the desiccating and harmful effect of the Waste Land with the restorative power of the cup, i.e., the Grail. In the Grail's presence Arthur himself is not only regenerated but his land prospers and his dominion spreads. However, all earthly glory has its term. After Perlesvaus has overcome his enemies and snatched the Grail Castle from a King of Castle Mortal, he himself follows the Grail to an Otherworld island governed by white-haired monks. Thus the proselyting, Cluniac ideal triumphs; and the chivalric world—though enlisted in the spread of the New Law—begins to fall apart: Lohout, Arthur's own son, is treacherously murdered; Guenevere dies of grief; an open tomb awaits Arthur at Glastonbury.

On the other hand, the victory of the spirit over the flesh was to be carried a step farther. Some twenty years later, across the Channel in France, a monk of the Cistercian order at Corbie composed the *Queste del saint Graal*. He wrote his work as a part of the great prose *Lancelot*, which we considered in our third chapter. He took up the religious theme from a hint made by his Glastonbury predecessor: the opposition of the New to the Old Law as set forth by the Bible. The Old Law or Testament had foretold the Christian dispensation in the phrase (he thought): *erit dux populi*

LADY CHAPEL, GLASTONBURY ABBEY

Galaad, which he translated "the leader of the people will be Galahad." This gave the author his clue. He would redeem Lancelot by giving him a sinless son, and he would make him the Grail knight in the place of Perceval.

Moreover, in making this change, he was obeying the spiritual dictates of his order. The Cistercians were the Platonists of the Middle Ages. Life to them transcended earthly experience. To attain the beatitude of the spirit, man must throw off the materialism of the flesh and become pure again in his soul. Had not Christ said: "Blessed are the pure in heart for they shall see God"? To let the Infinite dwell in the vessel of the Finite, as Augustine had taught, to bring the soul face to face with the Deity and allow it to flow (*liquescere*) into it, as St. Bernard preached, this was the doctrine of the Cistercian or White monks, and into the *Queste* one of their number poured his poetic faith.

As compared with the more solid *Perlesvaus* or Chrétien's more sophisticated Grail poem, the *Queste* appears sublimated in the extreme. Here all is light and shade, tones rather than arguments, traceries instead of outlines, expressed in attenuated form and with an upward thrust like the arches of Amiens or Rheims. In short, French Gothic in its best and most artistic period.

The plot, slight as it really is, springs from a Pentecostal frame of mind: the belief that on Whitsunday after the Resurrection the Holy Spirit dwelt among men. The event on which the *Queste* is founded is thus described in the Acts of the Apostles 2:1:

And when the day of Pentecost was fully come, they were all with one accord in one place.

And suddenly there came a sound from heaven, as of a rushing wind, and it filled the house where they were sitting.

And there appeared unto them cloven tongues like as a fire, and it sat upon each of them.

And they were all filled with the Holy Ghost, and began to speak with other tongues, as the spirit gave them utterance.

This scene the author of the *Queste* re-wrote in terms of a gathering of the Round Table. Actually he composed the Arthurian scene on top of the biblical one— in the manner of a medieval palimpsest, which is a parchment on which one writing is superimposed upon another. But where the Scripture referred to the Holy Ghost, the Cistercian always referred to the Grail; in such manner, however, that the allegory or double meaning is evident. Thus the Holy Grail now stands for the Third Person of the Trinity. In other words, it is the 'grace' of God, vouchsafed to the elect; and to 'see' the Grail is to see God, "not in a glass darkly," but "face to face" openly. I quote the Old French text in the translation by Lucy A. Paton:

And for that it was a high festival, the ladies came down from the palace to hear evensong, and when the king was come forth from the minster, he went up into the upper hall of the palace, and he commanded that the tables be set. And thereafter the knights went to sit each in his own place, even as they had done in the morning. And when they were all seated and were all silent, then anon they heard a blast of thunder so great and so marvellous that them seemed the palace would all founder. And right so there entered a sunbeam that made the palace sevenfold brighter than it had been afore, and all they that were there were as if illumined by the grace of the Holy Spirit, and they looked one upon another, for they wist not whence this brightness might have come. And none the less there was no one there that might speak or utter a word, and they were all dumb, both great and small.

And when they had bided thus a great while so that none among them had power to speak, but they looked each on the other as they had been dumb cattle, then there entered into the hall the Holy Grail, covered with white samite, but there was none might see who bore it. And it entered by the great door of the hall. And so soon as it was entered thereinto, the hall was filled with good odours, as if all the spicery of the world were spread therein. And it went through the hall all about the tables on one hand and on the other, and as soon as it passed before the tables forthright they were all filled before each seat with such viands as each knight desired. And when they all were served, then suddenly the Holy Grail departed, so that they wist not what might have become of it, nor saw into what part it went. And then they all had power to speak that afore might not utter a word. And the greater part of them gave thanks to our Lord for His great honour that He had done them when He had replenished them with the grace of the Holy Vessel. But of all them that were there King Arthur was the most happy and glad, for that our Lord had shown him higher favour than to any king that had been afore him.

Now of this grace all, both those of the King's household and those from abroad, were passing glad, for them seemed in truth that our Lord had not forgotten them, since He had showed them such high favour. And they talked so long as they sat at meat. And the king himself began to speak to them that were the nearest to him, and he said, "Certes, my lords, we should rejoice and be glad, in that our Lord hath showed us so great sign of His love that He of His grace was fain to feed us at so high a feast as is the day of Pentecost."

"Sire," said Sir Gawain, "there is yet another grace that ye know not. For there is no man but he hath been served with that whereon he thought with desire, but they were beguiled that they might not see the Holy Grail *openly*, for its true semblance was covered for them. Wherefore I here make a vow that on the morn without longer abiding I will enter upon the quest in such wise that I shall hold me out a year and a day and yet more, if need be, and never shall I return to court for aught that betide, till that I have seen it more *openly* than it hath been showed me, if so that I can and may behold it. And if that may not be, I shall return again."

With this setting before us, it is clear that, as was remarked above, the idea and the plot of the *Queste* are simple enough. Gawain, traditionally the brightest of the Arthurian knights, sees the problem and states it effectively. None of the knights, himself included, had seen the Grail "openly." What they saw was its shell:

Clothed in white samite, mystic, wonderful.

But its true essence had been concealed from them. Why? Because, for one reason or another, owing to some earthly taint, their hearts had been closed to the grace of God. Hence the quest, on which all of Arthur's knights now set forth. But hence also, the failure of that quest—in greater or less degree—for all of them save only one, Sir Galahad.

While the author of the *Queste*, in dealing with each knight's particular weakness (Perceval's is 'presumption,' Gawain's 'wrath' or 'homicide,' etc.), nowhere gives us a Joblike person, groveling in dust and ashes and beset by Behemoth, the entire role of Lancelot in his work is one long demonstration of the gravity of 'lust.' Lust—to him—is the mother of the vices, and to this sin he lets Lancelot sacrifice one by one most of his good qualities. The result was that, by a strange revulsion, a desire to embody his ideal at all costs, he fathered on Lancelot an impeccable and therefore colorless son, Galahad. His Galahad is a figment, not a human being.

But if our Cistercian fails us in this one respect, his success in other respects is remarkable. His book is not an easy one for us today to read. We no longer possess the requisite patience or the penetration. Above all, we lack the faith spiritually and factually that had made his soul glow. The nearest modern ap-

proach to his unworldliness is among the French Jan-
senists, and their date is the seventeenth century. Yet
it is precisely his sense of human values, the ways of
man compared with the ways of God, that makes the
Queste a great religious classic. And among the most
vivid impressions it conveys none are superior to his
treatment of Sir Lancelot and Sir Gawain.

The real hero of the *Queste* (and of the Grail-Lancelot cycle) is Lancelot. That fact I tried to establish in
my third chapter. It is Lancelot's problem which affects the author most, down to the tournaments and
deeds of valor that Lancelot must renounce, let alone his
attachment to the Queen. His is the great *rifiuto*, the
denial of all earthly glory. This is what the Victorian
poets never grasped—despite, as in the case of William
Morris, their sincere attempts at medievalism.

As to Gawain, the author of the *Queste* was an excellent Arthurian. He knew Gawain's role as Arthur's
favorite nephew and rationalizer. And he sympathized
with it. But as a Cistercian he was vowed to pacifism,
and Gawain was warlike and known, in the romances,
as the *chevalier à l'épée*, the "knight of the sword."
That Gawain would fail in the Grail quest was a foregone conclusion. On the other hand, he is represented
as the one among all the knights of the Round Table

intelligent enough to know what forsooth the quest is about and that he must share in it.

This brings me to my conclusion. If Greek art, in its plastic and poetic expression, is concerned with a finite creation, medieval literature—as seen in the Arthurian stories—represents an undefined one. A Greek temple or a tragedy by Euripides is determined by the mathematical law of 'dynamic symmetry.' That is not the case with a Gothic cathedral or an Arthurian romance. Here the imaginative content again and again outstrips the sense of external form, despite the geometrical design that controls such structures as Amiens or Notre-Dame or Rheims. Such a structure, whether architectural or poetic, must often be judged as to its separate features, not as to its entity. What counts artistically is the parts of the edifice: the architrave over the portal, the stained blue glass, the mass of flying buttresses, the exquisite sexfoil windows, the soaring Gothic arches. So it is with medieval romances; we are fascinated by the separate motifs, in their varying, diversified expression, not in the Arthurian cycle as a unity.

The main reason for this deficiency, if one so regard it, is that the Middle Ages are essentially an era of aspiration. This holds true in spite of the fact that metaphysically medieval men regarded the cosmos as

a fixed and established order. In allowing for an Infinite Being, whom no man can grasp—not even Galahad—they made of life a series of incomplete, though
not 'broken,' images. Rooted in the soil, in the waste
land of human error, they forced the human spirit to
aspire. In one of the later versions of the *Queste*, Gawain actually reaches the purlieus of the Holy Vessel,
and what is his experience?

Gawain [says the author] praised it much, yet might he not
know whereof 'twas wrought; for 'twas not of wood, nor of any
manner of metal, nor was it in any wise of stone, nor of horn, nor
of bone. And therefore was he sore abashed.

Had not Gawain himself instituted the quest? If now
he fails to achieve it, what moral is the reader to
draw? Obviously, that it is not the goal that matters
but the aspiration. Herein lies the universal applica-
tion of the medieval doctrine. But here lies also its
danger—the temptation on the part of the weak and
shallow to yield to the mystical process in a debased
form, as has happened time and again since the Middle Ages. On the other hand, among hardier souls,
among those to whom the rational faculty can give no
further answer, it has scored notable triumphs. As
that searcher after the Infinite, Blaise Pascal, was to
conclude: 'to know, is to seek' (*connaître, c'est chercher*),
And Pascal, by education and choice, was a Jansenist,

a descendant in the seventeenth century of the Cistercians.

As for the Grail, the official Roman church wisely never regarded it as other than a legend and therefore unorthodox.

In this chapter I am again indebted to the books by Newman, Miss Paton, and Bruce, cited before. On the *Perlesvaus*, of which there is an English translation by Sebastian Evans in the "Dent Library," see the edition published by Nitze and Jenkins (2 vols.; Chicago: University of Chicago Press, 1932–37). On the *Queste* see Albert Pauphilet, *Etudes sur la Queste del saint Graal* (Paris: Champion, 1921), and Etienne Gilson, *Les Idées et les lettres* (Paris: Vrin, 1932).

Additional material may be found in Joan Evans, *Monastic Life at Cluny* [1090–1157] (London: Milford, 1931), and in the works of Jessie L. Weston, accessible in any good university library.

INDEX

99